101
WAYS TO REALLY SATISFY YOUR CUSTOMERS

ALSO BY ANDREW GRIFFITHS

101 Ways to Market Your Business
101 Ways to Boost Your Business
101 Ways to Advertise Your Business
Secrets to Building a Winning Business

COMING SOON

101 Ways to Balance Your Business and Your Life
101 Ways to Network Marketing

101
WAYS TO
REALLY
SATISFY YOUR
CUSTOMERS

ANDREW GRIFFITHS

ALLEN&UNWIN

658.812
Pri

First published in 2002
This edition published in 2006

Copyright © Andrew Griffiths 2006

Allen & Unwin
83 Alexander Street
Crows Nest NSW 2065
Australia
Phone: (61 2) 8425 0100
Fax: (61 2) 9906 2218
Email: info@allenandunwin.com
Web: www.allenandunwin.com

National Library of Australia
Cataloguing-in-Publication entry:

Griffiths, Andrew, 1966- .
101 ways to really satisfy your customers.

Rev. ed.
ISBN 978 1 74175 008 9.

ISBN 1 74175 008 3.

1. Consumer satisfaction. I. Title.

658.812

Set in 12/14 pt Adobe Garamond by Midland Typesetters, Australia
Printed in Australia by McPherson's Printing Group

10 9 8 7 6 5 4 3 2 1

Contents

Acknowledgments

Customer service is an area that has fascinated me for many years, so I was pleased that my publishers, Allen & Unwin, reacted with genuine enthusiasm when I suggested this title to them. I had long dreamed of writing a book, so as I put the finishing touches to *101 Ways to Really Satisfy Your Customers*, my third book, I count myself very fortunate.

The response to my first two books has been astonishing. Not a day goes by when I don't get emails, faxes or letters from readers around the world thanking me for producing books that they have found, in their words, motivational, inspirational and practical.

As much as I like to feel that I am helping business owners and operators to succeed, this book wouldn't have been written without the help and support of many people. I would especially like to thank two groups of people.

First are those who have helped me to develop my writing skills: Ian Bowring, Emma Jurisich and Karen Penning at Allen & Unwin. A more professional and supportive team couldn't be found. They have encouraged me to do the best work that I can and they continue to play a very active role in my writing career. There are also many other people behind the scenes who edit and proofread the books, promote and publicise them, design the layout and, finally, print them. While I know that they often go unrecognised for their part in the process, I am very aware of and grateful for the part they play.

The second group that I would like to thank are the people I deal with on a day-to-day basis: my family, friends and clients. The pride I see in their eyes when my books are published means a lot to me. They understand that I may be a little reclusive when I have deadlines to meet and, without exception, they offer complete and unconditional support. I would especially like to thank Neville Burman, Andrew Burman (Internet guru), Phil Colbert, Cathy Lovern, Erwin Luthiger, Bruce and Julie Ann Stewart, Di and Kev Harris, John MacKenzie, Mick and Jess Dunn, Tom MacPartland, Noel Farquharson, Neil Swann and Charlie Holland.

Introduction

I am passionate about customer service. I find great customer service wonderful and I look for it constantly. On the other hand, I find lousy customer service infuriating and I see it every day. There is no doubt in my mind that those businesses that offer good levels of customer service have a far greater chance of success and growth than those that really don't care about customer service one way or the other.

I love going to a business and being surprised by excellent service. Every time I contact a business—either over the telephone, on the Internet, by writing to them or by walking through their front door—I can't help but do an impromptu customer service review. From my observations, we have all grown accustomed over many years to receiving ordinary service. So when someone *does* show an outstanding level of customer service, it's impossible not to notice.

Those businesses that have an honest commitment to customer service always seem to develop an army of loyal customers. These businesses grow by word-of-mouth advertising, and their customers stick with them through the good times and the bad.

Likewise, how many times have you sat down with friends and complained about a business that you visited that offered shocking service? As consumers we all spread the word about businesses that have treated us poorly and, now more than ever, we look for a recommendation from a friend before we make our final decision on where to spend our hard-earned money.

As business owners and operators we all have the chance to offer outstanding customer service, but it takes time and energy and a real commitment that has to be shared by everyone involved, not just the people serving the customers. I believe there is no better way to build a profitable business in any field or industry than by being absolutely committed to offering the highest levels of customer service possible.

This book will show you how to achieve this goal. It won't cost a lot of money or take an enormous amount of time, but it *will* take a strong belief in the value of customer service and the important role that it plays in the future success of your business.

How to use this book . . . and others in the *101* series

All the books in the *101* series are written in a style that will appeal to the reader who likes to read a book from cover to cover, as well as to the reader who likes to open a book at any page in search of an idea or a suggestion that they can implement today.

I strongly suggest that you keep the books handy and use them as a constant source of reference and inspiration. The ideas won't date and the suggestions and recommendations will work for practically any business.

The concept of the *101* series is to provide simple and reliable business advice from people with a strong background in small business. This gives the books a very practical advantage. Many people complain that the business books they have read in the past offer advice that is too difficult, too expensive or too time-consuming to apply to their own business. The *101* series of books takes into account that most small businesses have three traits in common when it comes to implementing new ideas and concepts: a lack of time, a lack of money and the lack of simple instructions on how to do it.

101 Ways to Really Satisfy Your Customers has been written in the same style as the other books in the series, *101 Ways to Market Your Business* and *101 Survival Tips for Your Business*. The books have four distinct sections.

Background information for those seeking a greater understanding of the subject

In *101 Ways to Really Satisfy Your Customers* this covers simple background information for those readers wanting to gain a greater understanding of the subject—in this case, customer service. It sets the mood for the entire book and explains some of my key philosophies and observations in the field of customer service.

The 101 tips, hints or suggestions

The main section of these books is the 101 tips, which provide simple, easy to implement ideas and strategies that can be of definite assistance to your business.

The tips in this book are divided into the following categories:

Section 1: Understanding your customers
Section 2: Your working environment
Section 3: Your staff
Section 4: Making it easy for your customers to buy from you
Section 5: The personal touch
Section 6: Face-to-face customer service
Section 7: Telephone customer service
Section 8: Promotional material
Section 9: Customer service and the Internet
Section 10: Following up on a sale is good customer service
Section 11: Internal customer service

Bonus section—20 more customer service tips

In *101 Ways to Really Satisfy Your Customers* the bonus section contains a further 20 of my favourite tips on customer service. They are some of the best pieces of advice that I have encountered regarding customer service and are a combination of all of the topics covered in *101 Ways to Really Satisfy Your Customers*.

Blank forms that can be adapted for use in your business

In *101 Ways to Really Satisfy Your Customers* the blank forms will prove beneficial for assessing your current level of customer service, establishing your philosophy towards customer service and maintaining a commitment to ongoing, high levels of customer service.

Getting a handle on customer service

What is customer service? It is both simple and complicated to define. I believe that any interaction with a customer is a form of customer service. There are, of course, the traditional forms of contact, such as a telephone enquiry, an over-the-counter sale, a letter or a meeting, but there are many others that don't spring to mind quite so readily when the topic of customer service is raised.

All forms of contact have an equally strong bearing on a customer's perception of a business and the overall degree of satisfaction they experience in dealing with the business. Sometimes they affect a customer on a subconscious level; other times they are more obvious.

Some examples of the less obvious areas of customer service include:

- Is it easy to find the telephone number of the business?
- Is it easy to find the physical address?
- Is it easy to find parking?
- Is the business inviting to enter?
- Is the business well lit?
- Are you made to feel welcome by the staff?
- Is the layout easy to navigate?
- Can the staff help with your enquiries?
- Does the business smell?

- Is the music too loud?
- Is the signage easy to understand?
- Are you treated with respect, or are you just another number?
- Do you have to queue for a long time to make a purchase?
- Do the staff have good selling skills?
- Do they make it easy for you to pay?
- Is the interaction with staff pleasant and sincere?
- Do they pay attention to the little things?
- Do they go above and beyond the call of duty?
- Do they thank you for your business and invite you back?
- Do customers leave the business wanting to recommend it to their friends?

There are many other questions that can be asked and, ultimately, they all deal with different aspects of customer service. Look at your business as a whole and I am sure that you will be able to identify many areas that you may not previously have considered as being customer service-oriented.

Customer service is really about satisfying your customers' needs and exceeding their expectations. It is a broad field with many variables that have been broken down into simple categories in this book.

The three secrets to really satisfying your customers

1. Take the time to find out what your customers expect from you.
2. Always meet these expectations.
3. Always try to exceed these expectations.

Understanding your customers and their needs

As customers, we all have certain expectations before we use a business. If you are going to a pizza bar, you expect that the pizza will be served with the toppings you specify, that it will probably take about 15 minutes to prepare, and that it will be packed in a box that will keep it warm until you get home. You will be charged a standard and acceptable price, and in all likelihood the pizza will taste reasonable. Subconsciously, these are all of the expectations that you have regarding this purchase. If the pizza bar meets them all, you will walk away happy and will probably return.

If you have been going to the same pizza bar for some time you may have developed a rapport with the employees, so if they mess up one or two of your expectations, you may forgive them. Perhaps you had to wait longer than usual, or they increased their prices and you were unaware of the change. Whatever the case, the degree of confidence that you subconsciously have in the business will determine how much you will tolerate.

If you are using the business for the first time, however, and they fail to meet even one of your expectations, it is very likely that you won't go back again (unless it is a completely convenience-based decision, such as the pizza bar is across the road from your home).

On the other hand, if the business exceeds your expectations—perhaps they gave you free garlic bread—and they delivered on every other expectation, you will go away raving about the business to everyone you know.

The two real keys here are identifying what your customers expect, and then meeting and, where possible, exceeding these expectations. This point is reinforced throughout this book as a key factor in understanding the customer service cycle.

Identifying your customers' expectations requires an open mind and communication with other people—your staff, your customers and your friends. What do your customers expect when they come to your business? Ask a lot of questions and put yourself in your customers' shoes. Look at your business from a customer's point of view and try to identify what they expect from you. Think about yourself when you make a purchase. Stop for a few seconds and go through the purchase process and the expectations that you have before you enter a business, and then try to determine if those expectations were met.

With regards to your own business, once you have a very clear understanding of what your customers expect from you, you can begin work on ensuring that you meet these expectations and, hopefully, exceed them. This book will give you plenty of ideas on how to do both.

Treating your customers with respect

Customers should always be treated with the utmost respect. Unfortunately, poor customer service generally stems from a real lack of respect for customers. As a consumer, I know that I'm not stupid. I know that my wife, my friends and my business associates aren't stupid either. In fact, it's highly unlikely that there are a lot of stupid customers out there, yet many companies still treat us as if we *are* stupid!

Treat your customers with the respect that they deserve and your business will benefit enormously. Don't get caught in the trap of looking at customers simply as numbers on a spreadsheet. This is an area where I feel many larger organisations have started to flounder. The unique needs of every customer are being lost sight of as businesses focus on their balance sheets and profit and loss statements. Customers know this and they have had enough. A flashy advertisement and a few false promises just don't cut it anymore.

Respect is a powerful word. Respect your customers' intelligence, their time and their decision to make a purchase from your business when they could have purchased the same item from your competitor up the road.

The benefits to your business of offering outstanding customer service

This is simple: if you offer really good customer service, your customers will keep coming back to your business. They will tell their friends, who will in turn visit your business, and they will tell their friends. This cycle of recommendations results in a business attracting more and more customers simply by word of mouth. Having people recommend your business isn't just a very good feeling; it's very profitable too.

Most small business owners and operators take a lot of pride in what they do. There is no better feeling than having a customer walk up to you and compliment you on the great business you are running. For me, this is the ultimate reward. For that reason, I always take the time to offer congratulations to any business that I feel is offering outstanding service. When a business offers poor service, on the other hand, I not only don't go back, I advise everyone I know not to go there.

So, the benefits to you of offering good customer service are that your business will grow by word-of-mouth (free) advertising, you will make more money, and you and your staff will all walk a little taller because you have positive affirmation that you are good at what you do. Sounds pretty good to me.

Ten common forms of lousy customer service

This is a hard one to limit to only ten examples, but the following are what I have observed to be the most common customer service mistakes. The aim of including a list such as this is to help you to identify where many businesses go wrong and, hopefully, to avoid making the same mistakes yourself.

Customer service can go wrong when:

1. Customers are kept waiting.
2. Promises are made but not kept.
3. Customers are treated like idiots.
4. Communication skills are poor (staff lack the ability to talk to customers).
5. Sales skills are poor (staff can't make a recommendation).
6. Service is inconsistent (good one day, bad the next).

7. It is difficult for customers to buy products.
8. Staff have poor complaint resolution skills.
9. Staff don't say 'thank you' at the end of the sale.
10. There is no follow-up on a sale.

You will have noticed that quite a few of the points listed above refer to sales ability, and there is a good reason for this. As this book will show, customer service is all about meeting and, where possible, exceeding your customers' expectations. Poor selling skills make the whole process so much harder; in fact, customer service suffers dramatically in businesses where the staff aren't well trained in the art of selling.

What customers expect when they make a complaint

We all make mistakes from time to time. When it comes to running a business, these mistakes can lead to a customer making a complaint. This is looked at in depth in the section entitled 'When things go wrong'. In this introduction I would like to point out the ten expectations that customers commonly have when it comes to having a complaint resolved.

By knowing what your customers expect, you may develop a greater understanding of the complaint process and of ways to resolve complaints quickly and fairly. Customers expect most of the following whenever they make a complaint:

1. To be treated with respect (acknowledgment that their business is important).
2. To be addressed by name in a courteous and sincere manner.
3. To deal with someone in authority who can resolve the complaint quickly.
4. To have the complaint taken seriously.
5. To receive an explanation of how a particular problem occurred.
6. To be called back when promised.

7. To be given progress reports if a problem can't be resolved on the spot.
8. To be given options to resolve a problem.
9. To receive a sincere apology when an error is made.
10. To be assured that the problem won't happen again.

As business owners and operators, it's easy to be defensive when a customer makes a complaint. However, we should all be grateful, because it gives us the opportunity to do something about it. Unfortunately, most complaints are never voiced; unhappy customers simply go elsewhere and tell their friends to avoid your business. Look at every complaint as an opportunity.

You need to know your competitors intimately

Ask a business owner why their business is better than their competitor down the road and you might hear: we carry more stock, we're cheaper, we offer better service, we're friendlier, we've been here longer, and so on. While these are good points of difference, they don't really inspire a customer to use the business. If you don't really know how your business is superior to your competitors', why should your customers prefer to deal with you?

I suggest that you visit your competitors. Introduce yourself and tell them that you just wanted to drop by and say hello and have a look around. A lot of people feel intimidated by this, but it's a useful thing to do. Talk to your family and friends to find out if they have visited this business and, if they have, what were their thoughts. Look at your competitors' advertising in newspapers, on television, on the radio, in the Yellow Pages and on the Internet. If they have a brochure, obtain a copy and compare it to your own. Look at the position of their business—is it more inviting than yours, or is the signage better? Can you improve what you are offering, or are you already better positioned than your competitors? Check out their staff. Are they well presented? How is their customer service?

There is a blank form in the Appendix at the back of this book that can be used as a guideline when doing a competitor evaluation. By doing this exercise you will be able to identify the areas where your business shines and these can become your main selling points. The next time a customer asks you why they should use your business, you can then answer them with your head held high and confidence in your voice.

Customer service passion (CSP)

Some businesses have it and some businesses don't—a passion for customer service is one of the foundations of a truly successful business. It's hard to say where it comes from, or how you maintain and develop your CSP, but without passion and commitment to customer service it just doesn't seem to work. It's like standing in a queue for 30 minutes and reading over and over the sign on the wall that says 'We value your business' or 'Our customers are the most important part of our business'; it just doesn't *feel* true.

Customer service passion is about doing the little things that show that your business is committed. Here are a few examples of CSP that I have come across recently.

A woman playing Scrabble on a commercial flight lost one of the tiles as the plane was landing. As she was getting off the plane, she mentioned it to the flight crew and gave them her business card, hoping that the tile would be found and returned to her but not really expecting it to happen. Within a few days she received an envelope containing the lost tile and a nice note from the flight crew. This simple gesture made the woman a staunch advocate of the airline.

On a visit to a drive-in restaurant a customer was kept waiting for what the manager considered too long. As a way of apologising to the customer (who wasn't perturbed by the delay), the manager didn't charge him for the meal. This unexpected bonus will long be remembered by that customer.

When I go to my local cafe, every once in a while they refuse to take my money, saying that as a regular customer they appreciate my business and this one is on the house. Why would I go anywhere else?

I recently made a sales trip to two capital cities. I had to hire a car in each city. When I picked up the first car at the airport, it was parked in the wrong spot, it was grubby, there was rubbish in the back, there was one street directory that didn't cover the area where I had to go, and the car hire was expensive. When I went to pick up the second hire car, which was from a different company, I was escorted to the car, we inspected it together to make certain that it was clean and in one piece, the attendant gave me a handful of maps and tourist information, and he explained what to do if there were any problems with the vehicle. I know who I will be hiring my cars from in future.

Customer service passion is a commitment. It has to start at the top of an organisation and work its way through the whole team. Everyone in the customer service loop needs to be made aware of what the business wants to achieve and of the level of customer service that is expected. A company might have great products at great prices, a simple and effective ordering system, friendly staff and so on, but it can be let down by one person on the warehouse floor who packs the goods poorly, or by a delivery truck driver who dresses like a slob, constantly has a cigarette hanging out of his mouth and has an attitude about where he will and won't make deliveries.

Customer service passion can be developed. If you can make your team see the benefits of offering excellent customer service, you will start to win them over. Of course, leading by example is the best way to illustrate this point. Show your staff your customer service passion and they will pick up on it. Soon it will spread through the entire business, becoming second nature to everyone. Your customers will definitely notice the change.

The future of customer service

I believe that we are on the precipice of a new age that I like to think of as the Customer Service Revolution. Technology is influencing our lives more than at any other time in history. But the technological advances we have experienced in the last twenty years are nothing compared to those that will occur in the next twenty years.

Customers literally have a world of choice. I buy products from the other side of the world on a regular basis. I do work for clients thousands of miles away simply with the click of a button. Things happen quickly and people expect fast service. Small businesses can look like large corporations with some smart promotional material and a good website.

As business owners and operators we all have access to new and developing markets and new sources of customers. It doesn't take a lot to start your own business. Pay a few fees and register a name, and bingo—you are a business owner and operator. This means that we are all facing increased competition, and I believe that the competition we face today is nothing compared to the competition we will face tomorrow.

As competition for market share becomes tougher, suppliers have to be highly competitive in their pricing if they want to stay in business. But the main thing that gives one business an advantage over others is customer service. Those businesses that are smart enough to realise that their future success lies with increasing levels of customer service will prosper in the coming decades.

The consumer backlash against having to stand in long queues in banks and other institutions, or against being put on hold for long periods of time, is allowing room for smarter operators to come in and develop their own market share simply by offering better levels of service at the same price. Customers today are time short and demanding. They know that they have choices, and they are prepared to take their business elsewhere if the service is substandard or prices aren't competitive.

I believe that more customers are lost through lousy service than through poor pricing. If people don't return your phone calls, don't deliver on time and don't thank you for your business, you will take your business elsewhere. And once a customer is lost, it's very hard to get them back.

So, while this is a testing time for many businesses, there are also enormous upsides. Customer service is one of the easiest and cheapest areas to improve in any business. Normally it involves just changing the way things are done. The tips contained in this book will give you ideas that you can start to implement immediately.

As the Customer Service Revolution continues, your business can either grow stronger and be a leader in your field, or it can be left behind to wallow with the majority of others. I would imagine that, since you have purchased this book, you already know where you want to be.

Recurring themes

There are a number of recurring themes in *101 Ways to Really Satisfy Your Customers*. The main themes are:

1. You need to know and clearly understand what your customers expect from you.
2. You need to know what your competitors are offering.
3. You need to meet and, where possible, exceed your customers' expectations.
4. You need to think like a customer.
5. You need to make customer service a priority.
6. Your customer service standards need to be reviewed regularly.
7. You must communicate with your customers.
8. You must focus on details and the little things that will make your business stand out.
9. You must deliver what you promise.
10. You must treat your customers with respect.

You will be reminded of the importance of these themes as you progress through the book.

1 | Understanding your customers

Customers are the one constant that all businesses need. This may sound blatantly obvious and it is, but one of the most common customer service complaints is that businesses don't listen to their customers.

We all need to take the time and energy to listen to what our customers have to say. We have to look for ways to make our customers feel comfortable, and to tell us their opinions on what we do well and which aspects of our business we need to improve. This first section of *101 Ways to Really Satisfy Your Customers* looks at ways of finding out what your customers expect from you, what they like and dislike about your business, and how to use these opinions to improve your overall level of customer service.

#1   Always put yourself in your customers' shoes
#2   What do your customers expect from you?
#3   Hire a mystery shopper to evaluate your business
#4   Observe your business objectively
#5   Take the time to talk to your customers
#6   Encourage your customers to give you their opinions
#7   If you ask for opinions, be prepared to listen to them
#8   Start a customer satisfaction survey immediately

1 Always put yourself in your customers' shoes

To be really committed to customer service, you need continually to put yourself in your customers' shoes. This simply means that you need to look at every aspect of your business from your customers' point of view. It can be easy to slip out of the habit of doing this and to revert back to an 'us and them' mentality.

Whenever you are making a key business decision that could affect your customers, stop what you are doing and think about all the possible ramifications. Write down the possibilities, both negative and positive, and then make your decision.

We all need to make difficult decisions in business from time to time; however, there is a right way and a wrong way to go about this. Simply putting up your prices with little or no explanation to your customers is a good way of upsetting them. Taking some time to explain that your prices will be going up and why the price rise is necessary will help to defuse the situation.

Start looking at everything that your business does as if you were a customer. You'll be surprised by how enlightening this can be.

2 What do your customers expect from you?

I have mentioned that the best way to ensure high levels of customer satisfaction among your customers is to know exactly what they expect from you and to ensure that you meet those expectations and, where possible, exceed them. This leads us to the point of finding out what it is that your customers expect from you.

The best way to find out what your customers' expectations are is to ask them. I believe that a simple flick-and-tick survey form can give you a lot of information. You want to know how important certain issues are to your customers, and from this you can fully understand their expectations. Your survey should ask your customers to rate the following items from very important to not important. (A complete customer expectations form can be found in the Appendix at the back of this book.)

How important to you are the following areas of our business?

Determining customer expectations	Very important				Not important
Easy parking	5	4	3	2	1
Trading hours	5	4	3	2	1
Range of products sold	5	4	3	2	1
Quality of products sold	5	4	3	2	1
The price of products sold	5	4	3	2	1
Overall level of customer service	5	4	3	2	1
Friendliness of staff	5	4	3	2	1
Attention to detail	5	4	3	2	1
Ability to answer your questions	5	4	3	2	1
Fast service	5	4	3	2	1
Familiar face each time you visit	5	4	3	2	1
Cleanliness of the business	5	4	3	2	1
Layout of the business	5	4	3	2	1
After-sales service	5	4	3	2	1

The more surveys you carry out, the more accurate the information will be. Clearly, you will need to tailor the questions to suit your particular business.

After your customers have completed a survey of this kind, you will develop a very clear picture of what aspects of your business they find important. This information can determine how you run your business and stop you making changes that could jeopardise your customers' satisfaction.

A good question to put at the bottom of the survey is: 'Do you have enough confidence in our business to recommend it to your family and friends?'

When asking customers to fill out a questionnaire of this sort, give them a little privacy and a place to do the paperwork. To ensure that it is confidential, have a box for responses (like a voting box) that they can slip the completed form into without having to hand it to a member of staff, as this can make some people feel uncomfortable. I also believe that it's a nice touch to give customers a small gift, such as a chocolate, as a way of thanking them for taking the time to fill in the form.

Customer expectations surveys can also be conducted on a website. I have found that fewer responses are obtained in this way than if you actually give someone a form while they are at your business premises. To increase the response rate, you could offer a gift or an incentive of some kind, but you then run the risk of people not being honest in their responses to the survey as they may feel that any criticism of the business will jeopardise their chances of receiving a gift.

The responses will identify exactly what your customers feel is important to them. Now that you know their expectations, you can do your utmost to ensure that you meet them.

3 Hire a mystery shopper to evaluate your business

As marketing consultants, we do a lot of mystery shopper surveys. A mystery shopper survey can take one of two forms. The first is where you employ a company to perform a mystery shopper evaluation on your business, and the second is when the mystery shopper is employed to do an evaluation on your competitors' businesses. Sometimes the two are combined.

By doing a mystery shopper survey on your own business, you can gain a clear and objective overview of the areas where your business performs well and the areas that could be improved. Normally a mystery shopper survey starts with a telephone enquiry and is followed up with a visit to the actual business. The information collected can pinpoint problem areas immediately. It's the old adage of having a fresh pair of eyes looking at a business. We conduct hundreds of mystery shopper evaluations every year and they have proven to be an invaluable marketing tool for the companies that have had them done.

Generally they sign up to have the surveys done on a regular basis, normally every three months, to check if problem areas are being corrected and to ensure that other areas that have surveyed well in the past are maintaining their standards. Restaurants, in particular, benefit from these kinds of surveys, but they are in no way the only kind of business to use mystery shoppers.

When using a mystery shopper survey to evaluate your competitors' businesses, the objective is to identify areas where they are weak and your business is strong. The end result is that you can focus your marketing on your own strengths, knowing that this particular aspect of your business is more appealing to potential customers.

There are lots of companies that conduct mystery shopper surveys. As always, the Yellow Pages is the best place to find a few company names to get you started. If you have limited funds and would prefer to get a friend to do the surveys for you, it is important to ensure that they compare oranges with oranges. When doing a mystery shopper survey, the surveyor needs to be 100 per cent objective or it will just be a waste of time.

If you are going to go to the effort and expense of doing a mystery shopper survey, you need to be open to the responses. It isn't the surveyor's fault if your business hasn't performed well, but it's a great opportunity to do something very positive.

4 Observe your business objectively

It can be difficult to be detached from your business and to look at it from an outsider's point of view. If you have owned and operated your business for a while, you are more than likely very passionate about it. You may be so busy doing what you do, that you can forget to take a few minutes out to be an observer instead of an active participant in all of the activities that take place on a day-to-day basis.

I have a friend who owns and operates two very successful restaurants. He often likes to dine at his own restaurants so that he can listen to what people say about the food and service. He doesn't eavesdrop, but he observes how the customers react when they are first seated, when their orders are taken and when the food is delivered. Of course, the staff know that he is there so maybe the service is a little sharper, but he does pick up a lot of comments that he can then act upon during staff meetings.

Take the time occasionally to be a fly on the wall. Sitting out the front of your business for a few minutes and watching what customers do may give you a few ideas on how to make the business more attractive. Wandering through your business with no intention other than to look around and observe can be very beneficial. Listening to the interactions between customers and staff, listening to what customers are saying about the business in general, and chatting to suppliers making deliveries can all provide excellent information that can be used to improve your business's overall level of customer service.

Observation is a powerful tool that is often forgotten in the clutter of day-to-day activity.

5 Take the time to talk to your customers

As a business owner and operator, it's very easy to spend your time in the back office rather than standing out front talking to your customers. People love to talk to the owner of a business— it's a mark of respect for you and for them.

No matter how busy you are, always take the time to talk to your customers. Ask them how they are finding dealing with your business. Get to know them and why they use your business. A few minutes' conversation with your customers can give you a lot of information. I find that if I stop and have a chat with my clients, I get to know them better and that strengthens our relationship, but it also inevitably leads to new business. Perhaps they were talking to someone who needs some marketing advice. Maybe I should give them a call . . .

When the owner of the business is too busy to talk to the people who pay the bills, there is a problem looming. It is important to remember that without customers, there is no business. I recommend that, occasionally during your working day, you stop what you are doing and take a few minutes to talk to your customers.

6 Encourage your customers to give you their opinions

We all need feedback from our customers. We need to know that we are giving them what they want and if there are any problems brewing. Every business should encourage its customers to give their opinions on their experiences.

The reality is that unhappy customers rarely take the time to complain about a problem. Instead, they simply don't come back. The challenge is to identify any problems before you lose them. Likewise, if there are things that you are doing that are succeeding in pleasing your customers, you need to know about them so that you can reward your staff and acknowledge their service, and thus ensure that they keep happening. So, how do you encourage your customers to give you feedback?

Here are some of the most effective ways to get feedback from your customers:

- Ask them—walk up to your customers, introduce yourself and ask them what they think about your business.
- Have a suggestion box—with a big sign and some pens and paper. Encourage people to write down their suggestions and ideas and to place them in the box.
- Have a questionnaire on your website—if your customers are likely to use your website, have a simple questionnaire on the site that can be filled in quickly and the response emailed directly to your business.
- Do a follow-up call after a sale is made.
- Send your customers a customer satisfaction questionnaire.

Some of these ideas are discussed in more detail in other parts of this book. The main message here is that it is very important to get feedback from your customers, and you need to ensure that this is made easy and non-confrontational for them. When doing any kind of survey, it's important that you give your customers the opportunity to remain anonymous.

You want honest answers, not just polite compliments. By asking your customers for their opinions, it shows that you value what they have to say and that will help to strengthen your relationship.

7 If you ask for opinions, be prepared to listen to them

If you are going to ask your customers for feedback on your business, you need to be able to review the information objectively, openly and, most importantly, be willing to act on it.

I have worked on a number of market research campaigns for businesses that wanted to gauge their customers' perceptions of their business. The results that came back were less than complimentary and, in some cases, downright terrible. When I reported on the findings, the business owner found every excuse in the world to justify the poor levels of service. Statements like 'Our customers are too demanding' or 'We are too busy to pander to every customer's needs' and, one of my favourites, 'If they don't like our service they should go somewhere else'. Generally, they do.

Very often businesses embark on the road to improving their level of customer service only to find it too confronting. They take negative customer feedback as a personal insult instead of a perfect opportunity to rectify problems that they may not have known existed. One way to avoid this is to have a plan in place that outlines what will be done with the information collected. This can prepare the business for the possibility of negative feedback, but rather than giving up in despair they will make changes according to the plan and work towards the desired outcome.

Often customers will want to know how the information they provide will be used. From my own experience, letting customers know that their responses will be used to improve the level of service encourages them to participate and makes them feel good because their opinions are considered important (which of course they are).

Every time someone gives you feedback that is less than positive, stop and think about how this individual is helping your business. Thank them for their honesty. Take their advice on board. If you have difficulty doing this because you are too close to the situation, get help from someone who can step in and resolve any customer satisfaction issues that your business may have.

I spend a lot of time going into businesses looking for ways to improve their overall level of customer service. When I meet proactive business owners and managers who are open to and very accepting of customer feedback, I always breathe a long sigh of relief. These people are smart and I know that their business will benefit enormously from their customers' feedback. Their willingness to take this feedback seriously and to act on it to improve the level of service they offer is a one-way ticket to profitability and complete customer satisfaction.

8 Start a customer satisfaction survey immediately

In the Appendix at the back of this book is a basic customer satisfaction survey. This can be copied and adapted to suit your business. I strongly recommend that if you don't already use a form like this, you start straight away. The idea of a customer satisfaction survey is to try and find out how your customers perceive your business and the service that you offer.

A customer satisfaction survey shouldn't be too long. Ten questions are more than adequate. Keep the questions simple and apply a grading system that is easy for you to use. Some businesses simply use 'Excellent' to 'Poor' in the response boxes; others prefer a numbering system. It's up to you. The technicalities of market research mechanisms aren't the issue here; what's important is how your customers feel about your level of customer service. If you give out 50 forms and 40 come back all saying that your service stinks, you might just have a problem.

Print the form so that it looks professional, and make it easy for people to fill in and return to you. I would suggest that you only print a small number of surveys at first because there will almost always be changes to the questions asked, which can be a problem if you have 10 000 printed surveys sitting under the counter.

If you are out and about and you see other companies' customer satisfaction surveys, grab a copy and compare their questions to the ones that you ask. Look for ways to improve the questions that you ask. I have a box full of survey forms from around the world that I use whenever I am planning a survey for my clients. Simple wording changes can have a big impact on the number of survey responses and the accuracy of the information collected.

With the advent of the Internet, customer satisfaction surveys can now be done online; and while the response rate is quite low, it does provide an extra source of customer feedback.

I always like to sit down with clients at the end of a project to have a debriefing. This is a face-to-face customer service survey, where we ask them to give us their perception of how the project went—both the good and the bad. This gives us the opportunity to address immediately any areas that the client isn't happy with, and it provides first-hand feedback on what the client liked about dealing with us. This is also an excellent relationship-building exercise. Our closing question is always 'Can we do business together in the future?' and the response is always 'Yes'.

Notes

_____
_____
_____
_____
_____
_____
_____
_____
_____
_____
_____
_____

Customer Service Action List

Things to do   **Completed**

1. _____

2. _____   _____

3. _____   _____

4. _____   _____

5. _____   _____

6. _____   _____

7. _____   _____

8. _____   _____

9. _____   _____

10. _____   _____

2 | Your working environment

There are many ways that you can make your business more appealing to your customers. While many of these may be obvious, there are also many subtle, service-related things that can make your business far more inviting and customer-friendly. This section identifies some of the best ways to improve your level of customer service by looking closely at your workplace. There are some excellent ideas and recommendations that will leave your customers impressed and very satisfied with your business.

9 Is it easy for people to visit your business?
#10   Is the entrance to your business inviting?
#11   Does the layout work?
#12   Instil confidence in you and your products
#13   Are there ways to speed up your customer service?
#14   Is the background music too loud?
#15   Cleanliness is essential
#16   Appearances deteriorate over time

9 Is it easy for people to visit your business?

Getting to your business is an important aspect of customer service. If someone has made the conscious decision to visit your business, you have to make certain that it's as easy as possible for them physically to get there.

Make certain that your business is well sign-written so that your customers can pick it out at a distance. Put your street address in a clear and prominent position at the front of the business. If you are upstairs or at the back of a building, ensure that the signage reflects this clearly.

If your business is new, try to find a landmark that is well known and that can be used as a reference point. Don't be concerned about promoting another business. If it makes it easier for *your* business to be found, then you are helping your customers. They are busy and don't necessarily have time to consult a map or to stop and ask for directions.

Is it easy for your customers to park when they visit your business? If it isn't, look for ways to improve the parking situation. Encourage your staff to park elsewhere so that they don't take up prime customer parking positions. Ensure that the car park is easy to enter and secure where possible. Are the parking spaces too close together, resulting in car damage and customer complaints?

Including a map on promotional material and even business cards is another way to make it easier for your customers to find your business. If you are thinking about opening a new business or relocating an existing one, this should be a key consideration when surveying for possible sites.

10 Is the entrance to your business inviting?

The entrance to a business can make or break it. If your business isn't visually inviting, your customers have a hurdle to overcome before they even think about making a purchase. The following are some of the most common problems associated with entries to businesses.

1. Cluttered premises

Do your customers literally have to climb over stock or displays to get into your business?

2. Poor signage

Generally, signage becomes cluttered over time. The name of the business should stand out above all other signage. Trading hours need to be clearly marked, and other signage should follow a pattern or a plan of some sort. Suppliers love to have their product name splattered over the front of businesses, and while this can be a selling feature for some businesses, it's important to ensure that it doesn't make the business appear confusing and messy.

3. The entrance is too small

Some businesses, especially ones with large numbers of customers coming and going, seem to have thrown all commonsense planning out of the window by making the front door tiny—to the point where only one person can enter or leave at a time. To the customer this can almost feel like walking into a trap. Our instincts take over and the fight-or-flight response can kick in, where you decide not to enter the business simply because it looks like it will be too hard to get out.

4. You're being watched

If the sales counter is facing the door, it can be intimidating to walk inside, especially if the person behind the counter watches every step you take. It's best if the counter isn't in a direct line with the front door; however, if it is and it can't be changed easily, staff should be trained not to watch people as they approach the door. Once the customer has come inside, a big smile and a friendly welcome will help to put them at ease. Instruct your staff not to stand around in groups talking and watching customers approach. This can be very intimidating, especially if the staff start laughing.

5. Is the front of the business clean?

A dirty entrance will deter a lot of people from entering the business, particularly if it is a food business. Cigarette butts, rubbish on the ground, overgrown gardens and overflowing rubbish bins can all impact on a customer's opinion of a business and on their decision to enter the business or go elsewhere.

6. Bad lighting

This is particularly relevant if customers visit the business at night, but some storefronts look dark even in the day. The entrance to a business needs to be well lit, both for legal reasons (in case someone falls over) and to increase the appeal of the business. Lighting around the outside of the building is also a factor, especially for safety. If the car park is poorly lit, customers may decide to go somewhere else that appears safer. Bad lighting is often simply the result of poor maintenance. A light bulb blows here and there, and before you know it the business is in darkness.

Do whatever is necessary to ensure that your business looks inviting from the outside. I have seen a lot of businesses that are quite amazing inside, but they struggle to get customers in the front door because the business looks so bad from the outside.

11 Does the layout work?

Is your business laid out in a logical manner? Is it easy for customers to find the products they are looking for? Are customer service areas well sign-posted and easy to find? Is it easy to find the front door when you are coming in, and is it easy to get out?

The layout of your business will have a major bearing on the overall level of customer service. I am sure that you have experienced confusion when visiting some businesses. Everything is hard—from finding the business, to entering the premises, to finding what you are looking for, right through to finding someone to pay for the purchase. If it's too hard, customers will go elsewhere.

Often this happens on a psychological level, where the business just doesn't feel right. It may look fabulous, but it just doesn't work. There are many professionals who specialise in identifying the correct layout for a business to ensure that it is customer-friendly, but many businesses still get it wrong.

As with many customer service issues, one of the best ways to determine if your business is well laid out is to ask your customers and your staff. Your customers may be prepared to complete a short survey, or you could just ask them a few questions. Your staff are generally the ones who answer customers' queries during the working day. Are they being asked the same questions time and time again, and if they are, is it a layout issue?

As with many aspects of your working environment, your layout needs can gradually change. The layout that you have today may no longer be relevant for the types of customers you have and their shopping patterns. The types of products that you sell and the quantity of products sold may also no longer suit your business layout, requiring it to be revised.

Make it easy for your customers to shop at your business. Ask other people for their opinions on the layout of your business and be aware that changes will need to be made over time.

12 Instil confidence in you and your products

With any purchase there is an element of risk to the customer. Will this product and the company I am dealing with meet my expectations? This is a fair question that needs to be answered, and answered well. I recommend that you use your business to fly your own flag.

If you have won any awards, put the certificates in a prominent place in your business, where all your customers can see them. This will reassure them and reduce any perceived risks associated with dealing with your business.

If your business supports local charities, display the certificates of appreciation. Likewise, if any of your staff receive an acknowledgment for outstanding service (such as employee of the month), put these notices in a prominent position. They show that your business is a good corporate citizen and that you care for the community and the people you employ.

If you have the type of business that can utilise a guest book or a customer comments book, leave it out for customers to read and to add their own comments. Whenever our company sends out a sales presentation kit, we include a list of past and present clients that will act as referees, verifying our company's ability to do a good job, on time and on budget. We also include written testimonials that clients have sent to us.

Put your company mission statement (see Tip #87) on the wall. If you are dedicated to offering exceptional levels of service, tell your customers this and be proud of the fact.

Look for as many ways as possible to reduce the risk factors associated with making a purchase from your business and you will increase your chances of making more sales and the overall level of customer service and confidence in your business.

13 Are there ways to speed up your customer service?

Serving customers quickly is very important in most businesses. Time is a commodity that many of us have in short supply, and it can be very frustrating to have our time wasted due to poor customer processing techniques. From my experience with customer service surveys, long delays significantly affect the overall level of customer satisfaction, and in many cases it's the number one reason for customers choosing to shop elsewhere.

Often, customer processing procedures have evolved over time. They may have worked in the past, but as the business has grown the old system no longer copes with the increased number of customers that the business may now be serving.

I suggest that you spend some time looking at your customer processing area. The following suggestions could possibly be incorporated into your business.

1. **Traffic control**
   Is it clear where your customers should go for service and how they should queue? There is nothing worse than a mass of people jostling to be served.

2. **Express service**
   Are there lots of people waiting for simple services that will take only a few seconds? If so, you may need an express service lane, similar to those found in larger supermarkets. Banks now offer express payment boxes for automatic deposits and bill payments. There are many businesses that could offer similar express payment options.

3. **The waiting area**
   Is the waiting area inviting and friendly, or are your customers forced to dodge other customers entering or leaving the business? Do you need to provide seats?

4. Distract your customers

Can you make the wait more interesting? I went into an insurance company recently to pay a premium renewal and they had a video playing with a well-known comedian telling jokes. It was fun and relaxing, and it made a five-minute wait pass very quickly. Best of all, I arrived at the counter with a smile on my face. Some businesses insist on having big clocks at the front of the queue so that you can watch every excruciating second pass as you continue to wait in line.

5. Review your signage

Look at your signage—just because you have a sign telling customers where to go and what to do, it doesn't mean that everyone will see it or understand it. Some of your customers may have reading difficulties or a language problem, or they may simply be distracted and not really observant at the time.

6. Talk to people who are waiting

When the queue is long, go out and talk to your waiting customers. Apologise for the delay and let them know that it won't be long. You might consider handing out a treat of some sort.

7. Cater for children waiting in lines

Children having to wait in queues can easily become distracted and bored. If your business has a lot of families coming in with children, look for ways to keep them entertained, such as a children's video showing in the background, a small playground, or some other distraction such as a fish tank (fenced off so that the children can't bash on the glass and send the fish into cardiac arrest).

There are many other areas that can be addressed that may be relevant to your particular business. The main aim of this tip is to encourage you to look at ways of speeding up the service that you offer and making any delays more enjoyable (or at least less miserable).

14 Is the background music too loud?

Have you ever gone out for a quiet meal only to find that the staff have the stereo pounding loud music into every corner of the restaurant? Background music can be very enjoyable, but loud music can be intrusive and a real irritant for customers.

There has been a lot of research done on the effects of music on customers. In the restaurant trade it is generally accepted that diners 'eat to the beat'. If you want your customers to eat quickly and move on, you play music with a faster beat. If you want them to take their time, perhaps buy another bottle of wine, play music with a slow beat. Similarly, classical music gives the subconscious impression that a business is expensive and of a high quality. So, playing blues music could have a greater impact on your bottom line than you might have anticipated.

Background music is being used in supermarkets around the world to encourage sales. Some supermarkets even go as far as playing music known to encourage people to buy specific products, down different aisles. I believe that over time, smart and effective use of music will become as important in a business as the lighting and general layout.

When it comes to playing music in your business, there are two main issues: the type of music and the volume at which it is played. Play something that is appropriate to your business. You may get a good response from the customers in your new age bookstore when you have Enya playing in the background, but if your staff prefer to play AC/DC when you are at lunch you will soon notice that sales decline at that time of day.

The same goes with the volume. If you're not sure if it's too loud, ask your customers. The music shouldn't interfere with conversation. After all, unless you own a music shop, your customers aren't coming in to buy the music. In fact, loud music is very disrespectful to your customers; it sends the message: 'We want the music loud because we enjoy it, and you'll have to live with it or go elsewhere.'

Show your customers that you respect them and appreciate their business by being mindful of the type and volume of music that you play in your business. If you have any doubts, ask your customers. If you are still unsure, play it safe with quiet background music that won't offend or irritate anyone.

15 Cleanliness is essential

There is nothing worse than going into a business that is dirty. Of course, it is hard to keep some businesses spotless, but there is a difference between being filthy and being messy in the course of doing your work. While it would be nice to walk into an engineering factory where the floor and machines are spotless, this may not be practical. However, if you were to compare two such factories, the odds are that one will be noticeably much cleaner than the other.

What is worse is going into a business that should be spotless, such as a restaurant, pharmacy, supermarket or bakery, only to see cockroaches and other vermin running around, food scraps on the floor, dusty shelves and dirty walls. Toilets are common areas for a lack of cleanliness. If I go to a restaurant and the toilets are filthy, I can't help but wonder what the kitchen is like and in all likelihood I won't go back.

The same applies to the staff. If the staff look dirty, the business gives the feeling of being dirty. We have done a number of customer satisfaction surveys in recent years for various companies and, without exception, cleanliness is considered one of the main prerequisites for retaining customers. This cleanliness applies to the actual premises, the staff and the facilities.

Customers expect clean businesses. Meet this expectation and you are well on the way to really satisfying your customers and increasing the chances of them coming back.

16 Appearances deteriorate over time

Over time, the appearance of any business premises can deteriorate, often without the owners or managers being aware of it. Whenever you go to the same place day after day, changes occur but they are less obvious than if they occurred overnight. It's like looking at a photograph of yourself now and comparing it to one taken ten years ago. Sadly there will be a few more lines, possibly a few more pounds and in my case a little less hair. If you woke up and saw that these changes had occurred overnight, you would rush to your doctor to find out what life-threatening illness you had suddenly developed.

Exactly the same changes can occur in your business. The day you open the doors the business is sparkling, the uniforms are fresh, the company cars look smart and everyone has a bounce in their step. Over the space of a few years, however, the premises can become run-down, the uniforms fade, the company cars become dented and old, and the signage and carpets deteriorate, giving the whole business a run-down appearance. A friend of mine aptly describes this as business fatigue.

Stop for a few minutes and take a good look at your business. Be objective. Think back to the day you opened your doors. How does it compare today with when you started? Are there areas that could be improved?

For most businesses, a revamp is required every five years or so. It may be necessary to get in a professional to give you a few ideas on what you can do to make your business sparkle again.

An added bonus with doing a review of this nature is that, as technology has developed, there are now many new and exciting options available when it comes to fitting out a business. There are some amazing new materials, communication systems, fabrics for uniforms and many other new developments that will help to freshen up your business's appearance.

The benefits to you are that this reinjection of enthusiasm and money into your business will be reflected in the attitude of your staff and the perception of your business by your customers. Customers like to see that a business is staying current and fresh. It shows a commitment to customer service that will pay for itself many times over.

We recently did a corporate makeover for a recruitment company. It was a very successful business, but their name stereotyped the type of recruitment that they offered. No matter how hard they tried, their customers only ever used them for one aspect of their recruitment needs.

We recommended changing the company name and logo, and completely revamping the office, staff uniforms, signage and company cars. The overall process required a firm commitment from the owners and I can really appreciate their bravery in changing the name of this well-known company. As it was, the change worked fabulously. The entire business was transformed and there was a real change in the attitudes of staff and clients. The end result was that this was a successful corporate makeover that will take the company into the next stage of its development. If the change hadn't been made, the business could have been overtaken by its competitors.

Notes

Customer Service Action List

Things to do	Completed
1.	
2.	
3.	
4.	
5.	
6.	
7.	
8.	
9.	
10.	

3 | Your staff

Staff are the front line when it comes to customer service. As customers we are very forgiving if a member of staff tries hard to meet our expectations, despite problems that are out of their control. For example, an excellent waiter will make a meal at a restaurant enjoyable even if the meal itself is fairly ordinary. The opposite of this is also true—an excellent meal can be ruined by a rude and incompetent waiter. This section looks at areas where staff can fail to deliver high levels of customer service and offers suggestions on the best ways to encourage and train your staff to go above and beyond the call of duty in looking for ways to really satisfy your customers.

#17 The meet and greet—first impressions last
#18 Treat your customers with respect
#19 Appearances count
#20 Take care with personal hygiene
#21 Communicate confidently with customers
#22 Ensure that your staff are knowledgeable about the products they are selling
#23 Smile!
#24 The basics are no longer basic—start at the beginning
#25 Take your staff to your competitors' businesses
#26 Take your staff to a business that you admire
#27 Have regular brainstorming sessions
#28 Debrief staff after good and bad experiences

#29   Encourage your customers to tell you if your staff give outstanding service

#30   Reward staff for outstanding customer service

#31   Ask a customer to come in and talk to your staff

#32   Give your staff experience in other areas of your business

#33   Teach your staff how to sell

17 The meet and greet—first impressions last

The meet and greet is one of the most important parts of the customer service experience. You and your staff will be assessed by your customers within the first few seconds and, rightly or wrongly, they will have formed an opinion about you and your business within that time. Of course, this opinion may change throughout the interaction, but you are miles in front if you do a good job with the meet and greet.

I suggest that every business review its meet and greet process. If someone walks into your business, is it very clear to them what they should do next? Remember that you see the same place, day in and day out, but for many of your customers it's all new.

I find it annoying to go into a business that is ambiguous about what you should do next. Should you go to the counter to place an order? Should you stand around feeling awkward until someone comes and serves you? Or should you start walking around the business until you find someone to help you? It can be very confusing if the business doesn't make this clear.

Motor mechanic garages can often be guilty of this, as are many restaurants. The customer enters the business and then has to stand around until someone comes over to them. In a garage lots of people walk around you, generally trying not to make eye contact. It would take only a few seconds to stop, greet the customer and ask if they need any help. Even if you get asked a few times, it's far better than not being asked at all.

In a restaurant there may be an awkward moment when you are uncertain about whether you should take a seat or wait until someone comes over and escorts you to a table.

Do you have a process for introducing yourself? For some businesses it may be appropriate that you actually shake hands to introduce yourself; for others it may be as simple as welcoming the customer, telling them your name and asking how you can help them.

However it works for your business, make certain that the meet and greet is fast, friendly and confidence-inspiring.

18 Treat your customers with respect

Treating your customers with respect is a theme that is repeated throughout this book, and for a very good reason. If you and your staff don't treat your customers with the respect that they deserve, they will go elsewhere. From a business owner's point of view, this can be financially devastating. It's important for staff members to realise the importance of respecting your customers and the ramifications if they don't (for example, they may lose their jobs because the business goes belly-up).

I often see businesses that have been fitted out at a cost of hundreds of thousands of dollars. They are situated in prime locations, and are well stocked with competitively priced goods. Everything is in their favour when it comes to succeeding, except there is a sales attendant behind the counter with a bad attitude. A sales attendant who ignores the customers or is disrespectful to them can cost a business a fortune in lost sales, both on the spot and with future sales. The state-of-the-art fit out and prime location are a complete waste of time and money if the person on the cash register has little or no respect for the business's customers.

Bad experiences create far more word-of-mouth advertising than good experiences. It's unfortunate, but it's a fact of life. As customers we have a very advanced and active underground propaganda network that identifies and singles out businesses that are notorious for providing bad service with a bad attitude.

As a business owner or manager, it's to your benefit to sit your staff down and explain to them the long-term effects of poor customer service. They need to be made very aware that their actions can impact on a lot of other people—namely, the other staff who may lose their jobs if the business isn't performing financially.

From my own experience, when you do sit people down and explain the ramifications of their actions they are often horrified, not realising the impact that they were having. Perhaps they were having a bad day, possibly due to problems at home. If you explain to them the long-term importance of treating customers with respect, most staff members will react positively and hopefully a change in attitude will follow.

Any member of a team with a bad attitude towards customers who cannot be reasoned with should have a short and very limited life in any organisation that wants to grow and be profitable.

Remember that every time a customer walks through the door, the first word that should come into everyone's mind is *respect*.

19 Appearances count

Looks are important. In training seminars I have this conversation with many people who argue that doing a good job is more important than looking impressive. While I agree with this in principle, I do feel that customers have a greater sense of confidence if you and your staff look the part. Going into a shop or restaurant and being served by a dishevelled member of staff gives the impression that they don't take their job seriously and, by association, they don't really care about the customers.

Imagine two electricians coming to your home to fix a fault. Electrician number one is wearing a neat, pressed uniform and carrying a tidy toolbox. She is well groomed and looks the part, which inspires confidence. The second electrician arrives wearing a crumpled pair of dirty overalls, with pockets full of tools and a cigarette hanging out of the corner of her mouth. Both electricians can be equally good at what they do, but it's far more likely that the first one will be invited back again because she looks more professional.

Looking the part shows that you want to impress your customers. You care about your appearance and you want your customers to be impressed. The same principle applies to company vehicles, the workspace, even advertisements and promotional material. It's all about looking the part. That is, after all, what your customers are expecting.

20 Take care with personal hygiene

We have all walked into a lift to be greeted by the waft of someone else's body odour, or encountered a hair stylist whose close proximity when cutting our hair makes the smell of garlic on their breath an unpleasant experience. It's very disturbing, to say the least. A recent study has shown that if there is one thing that most people would like tradesmen to improve, it is their personal hygiene—don't come to my place and stink it up.

There is a great story that I came across a few years ago. There had been a number of complaints about the level of hygiene of taxi drivers in a particular city. A national men's fragrance company decided to do a promotion where they gave every driver a bottle of after-shave and a deodorant to be kept in the taxis and to be used (sparingly) throughout the day. The promotion was a huge success and everyone was happy. Both companies got great national press coverage and the customers could once again get into taxis without holding their noses.

Personal hygiene is a key consideration when it comes to customer service. Of course, if you are a telemarketer it may be of less importance, but stop and have a think about the person sitting next to you and sharing your telemarketing booth.

If you work with food, personal hygiene is a huge issue. It can be difficult to discuss a personal subject like this and I would suggest that you make your expectations very clear when employing staff. Put it in writing and make sure that the new employee is very aware of how they need to be groomed.

An area that is often harder to break through is when it's the business owner who has a personal hygiene problem. There have been quite a few times when I have had to sit down with a business owner and suggest that the best way they could increase the number of customers coming to their business is to start using a deodorant. Some people take it well— others don't.

Once again, it's all about respect. By taking the time to show that you care about your personal hygiene, you are showing your customers that you take your job seriously. By association, you are also taking them seriously.

21 Communicate confidently with customers

Confidence is a tough one. Some people seem to have it and some just don't. Communication skills can be built over time; however, for a lot of people it's a lifelong challenge. Being confident enough to talk to customers doesn't mean that your staff should sit down with them and have a four-hour conversation about the effects of global warming or tell risqué jokes. It simply means that they are confident enough to interact with customers on the subject of their needs or wants in purchasing a good or service.

If any of your staff have difficulties communicating with customers, consider enrolling them in a personal development or public speaking course. There are a lot of courses offered dealing with areas such as starting a conversation, overcoming awkward moments, thinking of topics to talk about, use of voice inflection, and many more new and innovative areas.

Another interesting point to note here is that many people feel that they aren't confident when it comes to talking to people, but to other people observing them they appear to be incredibly confident and very effective communicators. I always remember an old friend of mine passing on some words of wisdom: 'What you perceive as your greatest weakness other people perceive as your greatest strength.'

22 Ensure that your staff are knowledgeable about the products they are selling

We can all relate plenty of stories about visiting a business to enquire about buying a specific product, only to leave dissatisfied with no answers to our questions. This is often the result of poorly trained or poorly informed staff.

Being able to pass on knowledge about the products that you sell is a big part of customer service. Your customers are coming to your business because they want answers to their questions. If they can't get answers from you, they'll go to another business that *can* provide answers.

This is a common problem in business today, with business owners being encouraged to employ younger staff so as to keep costs down. Their hourly rate may be lower, but so is their level of knowledge and their sales skills in general. If you want your business to succeed, give your staff every opportunity to learn about the products they are selling. Don't blame your staff for not knowing the answers to customers' questions if you haven't taken the time to teach them what they need to know.

Some businesses seem to be able to answer just about any question that you can possibly think of. Others struggle to answer the simplest of enquiries. Those that have the better ability to answer questions are offering higher levels of service, and I believe that in the long run they will be far more successful.

23 Smile!

Some people seem to struggle with the concept of smiling. It really is a basic principle of customer service, yet it seems to be an area that doesn't come naturally to a lot of people.

Nothing breaks down barriers more quickly than a big smile. If someone smiles at you, the natural response is to smile straight back at them. This is true all over the world and, as a rule, it can overcome language barriers and other communication problems.

You and your staff need to be able to smile. Before you pick up the telephone, smile; when someone walks into your shop, greet them with a smile; if you are sitting down to write someone a letter, write it with a smile on your face; when sending an email, smile first and then type. As crazy as some of these ideas may sound, a smile can be felt through a telephone line and on the pages of a letter.

Smiles are contagious. The more you give, the more you get. It's hard to have a bad customer experience when both parties are smiling at each other. I have often observed that smiles start to disappear towards the end of the day, or when things are really busy, or when money is a little tight or there are problems at home, and so on. I use the following technique to remind myself to smile.

Whenever I am about to take a telephone call or meet someone, I stop for a few seconds and think about what I'm going to do. This may be the first time I have met this person and I know that they will be judging me, both consciously and subconsciously, by my attitude. I clear my head of what has been happening throughout the day and I focus my complete attention on the person that I am meeting or going to be talking to. This works very well for me and makes it easy for me to smile and be friendly and to enjoy the interaction.

If, at the end of the day, you find that you have a staff member on your hands who can't smile at customers, you may need to think about their future within the company.

24 The basics are no longer basic—start at the beginning

I often hear people talking about the basics of customer service, almost in a way that assumes that everybody knows them. From my experience, very few people are really aware of the basics of customer service and, like virtually every business skill, they need to be taught.

You might feel a little bit embarrassed about telling a member of your staff how to answer a telephone or how to greet a customer, but if it's your business, your main focus needs to be on satisfying your customers and making sure that they have a pleasant experience when doing business with your organisation.

Many of the ideas suggested in this book are considered 'the basics'. I suggest that you encourage your staff to read it. This could be done in a round table format, perhaps chaired by you, the business owner or manager. Simply work through each section and each tip and make sure that everyone understands why it is important. This can be an open discussion, which I feel provides for a better learning environment, rather than sitting down and saying, 'You have to do everything that's in this book or you're fired'.

Customer service is a big issue and there is a lot to learn. I believe that you need to start at the beginning and work your way through all of the important topics, one step at a time. As every business has its own unique aspects, it is important to apply the principles of customer service in a way that is appropriate for your specific business. Sometimes it's difficult for people to make the leap from a theoretical example in a book to a real life, everyday situation that they may face.

One way to teach staff the basics of customer service is to team up new and impressionable staff members with a senior member of the team who can teach them the ropes. Be aware, though, that this can also backfire. The experienced member of the team has probably developed their own style, and it's likely that they are confident, that their product knowledge is good and that they know a lot of your customers well. The new staff member might mirror their behaviour, which may not be appropriate. They may become overly familiar with the customers, they may not learn about their products for themselves but simply repeat what the senior staff member says to customers, or they may learn bad habits and take short cuts without learning and understanding the basics.

For this reason, I suggest that all staff should have a very clear understanding of your basic expectations when it comes to customer service. You should control and monitor this. Once the basics are clear, introduce new and experienced staff members to add a different dimension to fresh and impressionable new staff. The importance of this orientation should be emphasised to the experienced staff members.

It is often a good idea to have your experienced staff sit in on basic orientations as well, as it's very likely that they have forgotten some of the basics. We all need to be reminded of these from time to time.

25 Take your staff to your competitors' businesses

I believe that this tip is particularly helpful for giving your staff a real appreciation of how your business compares to other organisations that are considered your competition. Before embarking on a field trip like this, take a few minutes to explain what you are hoping to achieve and what types of things you would like your staff to compare. Afterwards, conduct a debriefing to discuss the group's observations. How was the business that you visited better or worse than your own business? You may be surprised to hear some of their observations, and they will be interested to hear yours.

This exercise takes the myth out of what the competition offers in terms of service and products and makes it a reality.

26 Take your staff to a business that you admire

We all know of businesses that we admire. Everything they do, they do well. Just as it's a good idea to visit your competitors' businesses, it's also useful for your staff to visit a business that you really admire, regardless of what industry it's in.

I often find that businesses become a little stereotyped by their peers. Innovative ideas are confined to what the competitors do. While I believe that it's important to compare your business with your opposition, there are many other excellent ideas out there that can be adapted and used in your business.

If you go to a beauty salon and they have a great promotional idea, with a little smart thinking you can usually change a few details and use the same promotion in a lawyer's office or a restaurant or a mechanics workshop.

When taking your staff on a field trip to a business that you admire, talk to them prior to the visit about the types of things you would like them to observe. Have a good debrief after the visit and see what points they have picked up that you may have missed.

I am always on the lookout for businesses that offer exceptional customer service. Sadly, they are few and far between, but when you do find one of the best, think of it as a university for you and your staff to learn from.

27 Have regular brainstorming sessions

One of the most important lessons I have learned over my years as a small business owner and manager is that some of the best ideas for improving your business can come from your staff and other team members. All you have to do is ask for their input.

I recommend that you develop an environment that encourages input from all of your staff. One way to do this is to have regular brainstorming sessions. These should be conducted in an informal manner, with seniority within the business being put aside and everyone attending being encouraged to have their say.

I recently sat in on a brainstorming session for a client of mine. The business offered professional services to a large number of clients. The aim of the session was to identify where the business needed to improve its customer service. The person who offered the best input and the most logical suggestions was the receptionist. When you think about it, this is understandable. The receptionist spoke to all of the firm's clients at some time. She dealt with their frustrations, with unreturned phone calls, documents not being sent out on time, unreasonable waiting times in reception, and the daily mail. She knew which departments in the business got the most complaints, which individuals were the slowest at returning phone calls, and what the most common enquiries were from customers, and she had opinions on a host of other day-to-day matters. Her opinions were welcomed by the group, and her suggestions and observations were taken seriously. The end result was that virtually all of the business's customer service-related problems were eliminated following the two-hour brainstorming session.

Every member of an organisation has the potential to provide excellent input in areas that will ultimately improve the overall level of customer service. Welcome their ideas and suggestions and thank them for being involved. If you ridicule ideas or suggestions put forward, your staff will stop giving their input. These types of brainstorming sessions need to be well-controlled and chaired, otherwise it's easy to get side-tracked or bogged down on a particular issue. I always assign someone to chair the session, and when it starts to go off the rails, their job is to keep it moving forward. Some ideas may need to be followed up, and complex issues may need more than one session to be resolved.

28 Debrief staff after good and bad experiences

Taking some time to talk to your staff after either a good or bad customer service experience can be very beneficial.

With a good experience, it's an opportunity to praise a member of staff for their outstanding service, or perhaps to thank the entire team. We all like to receive praise and feedback, and it's especially powerful in a group situation. Taking it one step further is where the real benefit can come from this exercise. If you are discussing a good experience based on customer feedback, run through every stage of the sale or interaction. Highlight where the encounter shone and set some goals. Make this the norm rather than an exceptional case. By explaining to your staff the benefits that everyone receives from happy customers and encouraging every member of your team to aspire to this same level, you can boost your entire customer service.

A bad customer encounter is an opportunity to highlight potential problems with your business and to identify ways to overcome them. The debrief following a bad experience shouldn't be a witch hunt; normally, if someone has messed up, they know it and are generally apologetic about it. If they aren't, the complaint has just become more serious and needs to be discussed behind closed doors.

During the bad experience debrief, look at every stage of the interaction. Where did it go wrong? What should have been done to prevent the situation becoming a complaint? The debrief needs to be conducted in an open environment that welcomes input from everyone involved.

The aim of conducting any debriefing is to look for ways to improve the level of service that you are offering to your customers.

29 Encourage your customers to tell you if your staff give outstanding service

A lot of the focus on customer service is aimed at encouraging your customers to give you feedback about virtually every aspect of your business. This feedback is nearly always constructive, as it is to do with ways in which you can improve your overall level of customer service. While this is extremely important, there are also times when we all like to get a pat on the back and a nice piece of positive reinforcement that tells us we are doing a good job.

I suggest that you encourage your customers to let you know if any member of staff goes above and beyond the call of duty and offers really outstanding service. You may want to ask your customers about this while they are visiting your business. You may wish to start an Employee of the Week or Employee of the Month award, as voted by your customers. There are lots of options, but however you want to do it, let your customers be involved. After all, they are the ones who should be judging your overall level of service.

Rewarding your staff for providing excellent customer service is discussed in the next tip.

30 Reward staff for outstanding customer service

If you implement the ideas in this book, you will get a lot of feedback from your customers. Some of this feedback will single out particular individuals for being good service providers and you may need to develop ways to recognise and reward these staff for their efforts.

Rewarding staff for outstanding customer service is a very good way to ensure that it keeps happening. Too many businesses only reward staff for specific sales results, while completely ignoring the area of customer service. I also hear a lot of business operators complaining about having to reward staff simply for doing their job. Unfortunately, we all work better with a little incentive—it's simply human nature.

Staff can be rewarded in many ways for offering quality service. Often simply acknowledging that an individual has done an excellent job is enough, especially in front of their peers; however, there are many other ways to thank and reward your staff.

Rewards can take the form of financial incentives such as a bonus or a gift offered in recognition of quality customer service. If you are giving a gift, put some thought into it. Try to give something that the staff member will really appreciate and remember.

Other kinds of recognition can include special treatment, such as a longer lunch break or a later starting time for a week. Perhaps they can choose their own roster, or you could give them an assignment that will be a fun project to work on.

31 Ask a customer to come in and talk to your staff

This is an interesting technique that I have seen work very well. Just talking to your staff about what you are trying to achieve with your business may not have the impact you are looking for. After all, they see you every day, they might be a little afraid of you as the 'boss', they might not relate to you, or they simply may not grasp the importance of what you are trying to get across to them.

The best way to get everyone to sit up and take notice is to get a regular customer to come in and talk to your staff about what they like about the business and what they don't like. It may be hard to find someone to do this, but most businesses have a few customers who are very vocal and willing to give some feedback.

This feedback session is designed to highlight the areas where the business offers good service and those areas where it needs to improve. Your staff will listen with considerably more attention, because (hopefully) they will have an instinctive respect for the customer. Issues that you may have been trying to resolve for months will be fixed almost overnight when discussed from a regular customer's point of view.

As always, if you are inviting someone to come into your business and to be open and forthright, you need to be prepared to take their comments on board. The areas that need improving are equally as important as what the customer likes about your service. This is an excellent way to deal with issues that you may have been struggling with for some time.

32 Give your staff experience in other areas of your business

Job swapping is a relatively new concept that has a lot of merit. The idea is to move staff within your business into different roles so that they get a greater understanding of the role that everyone plays. How does this affect customer service?

This temporary job swapping gives all members of staff a greater understanding of and empathy with the key challenges that other staff members face in their day-to-day work duties. It helps to reduce the attitude of 'It's not my job to do that' and reduces complaints about other departments within a business.

It's easy to assume that the people in despatch at a factory are responsible for shipping delays that result in customer complaints. However, if you spend a day packing and despatching hundreds of orders yourself, you may develop a greater appreciation of the job and of the whole despatch process. You may have some ideas and suggestions that could improve the overall despatch process and you will definitely be more able to explain to potential customers how it works and to give them a realistic time frame for delivery.

Too often people blame other members of staff when customer complaints arise. They may be quite justified in doing so. However, by having a better understanding of the other areas within a business, there is no doubt that the entire organisation will work more as a team, rather than as an 'us and them' organisation.

The main aim is always to ensure that the customers receive the best level of service possible. Job swapping enables service to be improved simply by increasing awareness. It takes people out of their comfort zones and forces them to play a more active role in an organisation.

33 Teach your staff how to sell

Good selling skills are necessary to really satisfy your customers. Now, I certainly don't mean that good selling skills are high-pressure selling skills—in fact, quite the opposite. There are stages to a sale that will make the whole encounter far more professional for all involved, and the bonus is that your customers leave happy (and your business becomes more profitable).

Most sales follow the stages listed below:

1. The meet and greet.
2. Qualifying your customers' needs (asking questions).
3. Determining the most important prerequisite (price, delivery, brand, guarantee).
4. Making recommendations.
5. Closing the sale.
6. Following up the sale.

This is a simplified version of a somewhat complex process, and while it may not be relevant to all businesses it will generally apply to most. Training is available at all levels, from introductory sales skills to more involved training in one particular aspect of the sales process, such as closing the sale or qualifying your customers' needs.

By giving all of your staff the skills and knowledge necessary to be able to sell professionally, your customers will be impressed and they will be far more likely to buy your products.

There are countless institutions that offer sales training. Choosing which one to use can be difficult, but I take the approach that the one that sells the best pitch to you is probably the one to use, for obvious reasons. It's wise to ask the training organisations about their background and experience, and I always ask for references from past clients to verify their abilities. If a training organisation isn't prepared to offer this information, look elsewhere.

To be effective, training needs to be conducted regularly. It's not a one-off scenario. To get the most benefits, institute a long-term training plan and commitment. I also suggest asking your staff about the areas that they would like to be trained in.

Notes

Customer Service Action List

Things to do   **Completed**

1.

2.

3.

4.

5.

6.

7.

8.

9.

10.

4 | Making it easy for your customers to buy from you

I struggle with the fact that many businesses subconsciously (and sometimes consciously) put barriers in front of their customers that make it difficult for them to make a purchase. Customer service is about making it easy for people to buy from you. Don't wait until a competitor opens up next door and makes it easier for potential customers to buy from them. Be proactive and take control today. This section looks at the best ways to remove the most common barriers to a sale and suggests ways to make it easy for your customers to buy from your business. The end result is that your customers will be happier and they will definitely be well on the way to complete satisfaction.

#34   Offer the right products
#35   Make sure that your pricing is correct
#36   Make it easy for customers to pay you
#37   Eliminate all obstacles to making a purchase
#38   Are your trading hours customer-friendly?
#39   If necessary, go to them

34 Offer the right products

I have observed that there are two distinct kinds of businesses. The first type seems to go out of its way to make shopping a problem. Whatever you want they don't have, but they can order it in. The staff are disinterested, the layout is worn and uninviting, the business may smell old and musty, even if it isn't that old, and every time you leave that business you feel dissatisfied.

The second type of business is fresh and energetic, whatever you ask for they have, finding the product that you want is easy, and the staff are always friendly and enthusiastic.

These two types of businesses are both very common. Clearly, the second is far more inviting and there is a much greater chance that you will return to it than to the first type.

I recently went into an electronics shop to buy a power adapter for a computer attachment. All I wanted was to walk in, buy the product and walk out. Instead, what unfolded was a nightmare. The business I chose to visit markets itself as having absolutely everything electronic. When I asked the bored-looking young man behind the counter if they had the relevant power pack, he simply said 'no' and went back to his newspaper. I found this incredibly irritating, so I stood there waiting for him to get the message. After a few minutes, he looked up again and asked if there was anything else that I wanted. I repeated my request and he called out for the techno wizard hiding out back to come and sort me out. (His exact words were, 'There's some guy here who wants something and I don't know what he's talking about.' Smooth, very smooth.)

The wizard came out and, while he was polite enough, the scenario that unfolded was hilarious. He started giving me electronic kits that I could 'easily' assemble at home. All I wanted was a plug-in power pack, but now I was standing in this store with my arms full of electronic gizmos, soldering irons, instruction booklets and stuff that I'm sure was developed by NASA. I burst out laughing and said to the guy that he had to be joking. Then he proceeded to lecture me on how easy it was to put it all together and surely I had the ability to do something as 'simple' as this.

For those that know me, if I need a light bulb changed I call in an electrician—believe me, it's safer for all parties this way. My wife is the handy one in our relationship and I'm proud to admit it. The ongoing irony of the situation refuelled my laughter and, of course, the wizard assumed that I had gone insane. Finally, I put everything on the counter and walked out and up the road to another store that sold me a power pack for $29.95, with the whole transaction lasting less than a minute. The really dumb thing on my part was that I had been to the first electronics store a number of times before with a similar outcome, but I persevered because I simply couldn't accept that they could keep getting it so wrong time after time.

You may be able to relate to this story and have had similar experiences. Understanding your customers and knowing what they need is the essence of customer service. Clearly, you are not going to be able to provide the exact product for every customer that comes in your door, but you should be able to provide the right products for the majority of them.

Further to this, you need to be generous enough to help the customer find the right product, even if you can't sell it to them. Try to point them in the right direction, make a quick call, or give them the telephone number of a business that might be able to help them, even if it's the opposition. By doing this, you have still offered good customer service even though you didn't make a sale, and the customer will remember your willingness to help.

35 Make sure that your pricing is correct

Pricing is always an important issue for customers. No one likes to feel that they are being ripped off. I really believe that most customers are prepared to pay a little more for a product if it's more convenient to buy from a particular business or if the service is generally better. But there is a limit.

Setting prices is difficult. Having a price rise is also a touchy point. When setting your prices there are a number of factors to be considered. How much does your competition charge for the same product? If you don't know, you should find out. Is the product that you are offering better? Are there realistic reasons that could enable you to charge more? Consumers today have a lot of choice, so if you are going to charge more you really need to be able to justify it. Likewise, if you are going to price yourself low, so that you undercut your competition, is this sustainable? Will your business be able to survive at these lower prices and consequent lower profit margins?

You need to make a conscious decision about how you want to attract your customers. Ideally, you may be able to win them over on price and service, and this is a good objective. But many businesses are able to charge a premium because they have a long history of being good at what they do, or they may stock a premium product that is in demand, regardless of price. Put simply, if you aren't trying to attract customers based purely on price, your service needs to be very good.

Deciding to raise prices is also a difficult dilemma. Prices have to go up—as consumers we are very aware of this point, but we still don't like it. I witnessed this in action recently. In Australia a goods and services tax of 10 per cent was introduced a while ago. I was in a health food shop for a meeting (believe it or not) on the first day of the new tax regime. The business had decided that today they would add the tax, as well as their own price rise, to the cost of all their products. The result was that a drink went from $3.00 to $3.60 overnight. That morning there were a lot of unhappy people storming out of the business, telling the owner that they wouldn't be returning. The new tax was understandable, but the other price rise was simply too much for the customers to accept.

Many businesses increase their prices without really thinking it through. The health food business mentioned above quickly lowered their prices, but the damage had already been done.

Talk to your customers and explain any price rises. If your costs have gone up, explain this and ensure that you can justify your proposed price rise. Customers can accept logical price rises. It's also easier for them to accept more regular small price rises than one big one every few years.

36 Make it easy for customers to pay you

I have spoken about this point many times in my other books and at seminars. Some businesses just seem to make it really hard for their customers to pay for their purchases. Here are some common problems in this area:

1. Long queues to make a payment
We all hate having to stand in long lines to give someone our hard-earned money. Queues seem to be getting longer, not shorter. Look for ways to speed up the payment process.

2. Not accepting all payment options
We generally assume that all businesses will accept all credit cards these days, but this isn't a fair assumption. It can be very embarrassing to arrive at the cashier's desk only to find that they don't accept the credit card that you wanted to pay with (or the only one you have on you). Some businesses even seem to run into problems with taking cash off their customers. The more payment options that you can offer, the easier it will be for your customers to do business with you.

3. Complicated payment procedures
Some businesses have developed complicated payment procedures that require a long time to process. The customer has to stand at the cash register waiting while forms are filled in, credit card numbers are typed in manually, questions are asked, and so on. These businesses are dinosaurs; in the new electronic age, there is no excuse for long, drawn-out and overly complicated payment procedures.

Often payment procedures have evolved over time and the system being used today is no longer efficient or relevant. I always recommend that payment procedures for customers are reviewed on a regular basis to find ways to make the system work better and faster. Make it quick and make it simple, and your customers will appreciate it.

37 Eliminate all obstacles to making a purchase

I talk about coffee shops a lot. There are two reasons: the first is that I spend a lot of time scribbling notes in coffee shops, and the second is that they often produce customer service anecdotes that can be applied to virtually every kind of business.

I visited a coffee shop recently that just couldn't seem to get it right. The shop itself was fabulous, the location was great, and even the coffee was good, but they had absolutely no idea about customer service. To order your coffee you had to stand in a line that moved at a snail's pace. The staff working the till had to punch so many buttons I thought they must have been writing a novel. After they had taken your order you then had to wait by the counter with the rest of the crowd for your coffee. The silliest part was that there was no way to know whose order was whose. They put a cappuccino on the counter and yelled out 'One cappuccino.' Of course, everyone there ordered one cappuccino, so whose was this one?

The whole process was a mess. People were arguing, the staff had no idea whose order was whose, and the whole time the owner sat at a table and watched the mess unfold. Who is ever going to go back to the counter to order a second coffee and go through all that again? How simple would it be to give people a number? I still don't understand the reasoning behind this coffee shop's service philosophy, but it's a great way to learn what *not* to do.

This business made it really hard to make a purchase. Many businesses inadvertently put as many obstacles as possible in the way of their customers buying their products. It may be a cluttered counter, or a prerequisite that you purchase a minimum amount of a product. Perhaps you are made to wait on the end of the telephone for half an hour for the privilege of handing over your money, or it may simply be too complicated for a customer to get served.

Whatever the reason, a key to customer service is to remove all obstacles that make it harder for your customers to make a purchase from your business. Every step of the buying process should be as smooth as silk.

38 Are your trading hours customer-friendly?

Trading hours can be a touchy point for many customers, as well as for many businesses. I live in a tourist-oriented city, where a large proportion of the workforce aren't employed in 9 to 5, Monday to Friday, positions. As a result of this, many businesses that would traditionally be closed on weekends are open to provide a service to the thousands of people employed in the hospitality and tourism industry.

Setting your opening hours is all about achieving a balance between offering a convenient service for your customers and ensuring that your business is profitable. Some businesses are open for too many hours a week, making their labour costs very high. A prime example of this is the introduction of Sunday trading for retail shops. The aim of this is to encourage more people to shop more often. However, what can happen is that the same number of people shop at the business over a longer period of time, resulting in the same income being generated by the business, but they have the extra costs associated with one more day's trading. Not a good outcome for the business. Hopefully the business will build up and attract more customers and so increase their income as a result of this extra day of trading.

As always, talk to your customers about your trading hours. If you were open longer would that encourage them to visit your business more often? Would it be of benefit to them if you opened earlier or stayed open later? These are the questions that you need to be asking your customers. Open lines of communication with your customers will provide answers to any questions that you may have regarding your business.

39 If necessary, go to them

In recent years there has been a significant increase in the number of businesses that go directly to the customer, and I believe that this trend will continue. We all tend to struggle with time, and so any business that can save us time will definitely be considered a customer service leader.

A friend of mine runs a home-based business and doesn't drive. The dry-cleaning business she uses picks up clothing from her home and delivers it, freshly laundered, to her door. She wouldn't consider using anyone else.

Are there ways that your business could take your products or services directly to your customers? Here are a few other examples that I have come across recently:

- Mobile battery sellers—they come to you when you get a flat battery.
- Mobile mechanics—they come to you to work on your car.
- Mobile dog washers—no more wet dogs in the car.
- Mobile finance brokers—they discuss your finance needs in your own home.
- Restaurants—home delivery is becoming more popular by the day.
- Hairdressers—many will now come to your home or office.

These are just a few examples of businesses that traditionally ran from a fixed location but realised the potential benefits of taking their products and services directly to their customers and profited as a result. Perhaps there is some way that your business can go directly to your customers. I have noticed in the marketing and public relations fields that I now spend much more time in my clients' offices than in the past. I am more than happy to do this, as it gives me a better understanding of their business and helps to develop our relationship.

Making life easier for your customers is a key success strategy when it comes to customer service. Look for as many ways as possible to achieve this and your customers will be more than satisfied with your business. Remember, though, that if you are going to offer this service, tell as many people as possible about it. There is no point in being a customer service guru and not telling your customers about it.

Just because a mobile service hasn't been tried in your business before doesn't mean that it won't work. Be innovative and look to be the first to establish a business that goes directly to your customers.

Notes

Customer Service Action List

Things to do   **Completed**

1.
2.
3.
4.
5.
6.
7.
8.
9.
10.

5 | The personal touch

I believe that the personal touch can make all the difference when it comes to exceeding your customers' expectations. Looking for ways to offer the personal touch requires a degree of effort, but the rewards can be huge. Think about the businesses that you visit the most, the ones that you really like and that you recommend to your friends. The odds are that these businesses have that special something, and it is likely to be the personal touch. This section will look at some of the best ways to improve your overall level of customer service by offering the personal touch.

#40   The sweetest sound is your own name
#41   Reward customers for coming back
#42   Be one step ahead of your customers
#43   Show that you are proud of your business
#44   Remember important dates
#45   Make a visit to your business memorable
#46   Start a VIP club
#47   Be patient and courteous with your customers

40 The sweetest sound is your own name

One of my favourite business gurus is Dale Carnegie. His observations on personal behaviour and self-development are legendary. In his most famous book, *How to Win Friends and Influence People*, he mentions a point that has stuck with me for many years: the importance of remembering a person's name and using it whenever you meet them.

This is no small feat, especially if you have a business that has thousands of customers. What you can do, though, is to encourage your staff to use customers' names after they have made a credit card purchase: 'Thank you, Mr Jones. Is there anything else that I can help you with today, Mr Jones?' By using a person's name you are showing them that they are not just a credit card with a pair of legs attached.

There are many times during an exchange when a customer may give you their name. If it's a telephone enquiry, it's normal courtesy to say who is calling. The customer's name should be noted and used throughout the conversation. I may be a little old-fashioned, but I encourage my staff to use formal titles such as Mr and Mrs when talking to someone they are not familiar with. If the customer says that they should call them by their first name, that's fine. Respect has been shown and continues throughout the conversation.

Some people have difficulty remembering names, but there are a number of techniques for making it easier. I have mentioned in my earlier books the technique I use, but I will mention it again here because it works so well for me. It's called memory association. Whenever I meet a person for the first time, I put a picture of them in my mind and I think of another person that I know well with the same name. For example, if I meet a man called Jamie, I associate him with a great friend of mine called Jamie. Whenever I see this man, the picture of Jamie comes into my mind and I remember the man's name. It works well for me and it has worked well for many of the people I have told about this technique.

Another excellent technique is to use the person's name repeatedly in the first few conversations so that you get used to saying it. After a while, you will have trained your mind to remember that name and it will come automatically without you even having to think about it.

It can be embarrassing when you forget someone's name. In this case, the chances are they have forgotten yours as well, so just get it over with and ask them.

I have also developed a habit from some years ago when I did a lot of travelling overseas for work and I was meeting a lot of people. After a sales trip I might have 100 new business cards in my folder. How on earth could I remember all of these people? I started to do something which has proven to be very valuable, even ten years down the track.

Following a meeting with a new person, I sit down for a few minutes and write some details on the back of their business card. It might be something about the person that will jog my memory—perhaps they have purple hair. It might be something in their office that I can associate with them, perhaps a picture or a trophy or a book. There might have been something memorable in the conversation. I just jot down a few points and then, when I go through my teledex of business cards, on reading the back of any card I know exactly who that person is and a few details about them. Now I know that if they were to ring me or if I bump into them, I will remember their name.

Do whatever works for you, but try to remember your customers' names. Encourage everyone in your business to get into the habit of respectfully using your customers' names and the end result will be happy customers.

I also believe that customers like to know the name of the person serving them in a business. Because of this, I am a believer in name tags, particularly in retail-style businesses. Some people really don't like the idea of name tags (I have no idea why not), but it's a personal decision that I believe can make a difference when it comes to customer service.

41 Reward customers for coming back

In simple terms, a loyalty program is a structured way of saying 'thank you' for using a business on a regular basis. As a bonus, they actively encourage customers to keep using a business in order to claim prizes or rewards for being loyal. The most well-known loyalty programs are frequent flyer campaigns and credit card membership rewards. Loyalty programs can be developed for just about any business, and they certainly don't apply just to large corporations.

If you have customers that use your business regularly, reward them—they are your best form of advertising. In today's modern business environment, failing to recognise and appreciate that your customers are regulars can easily cause them to move their business somewhere where they will be appreciated.

Loyalty programs can take many different shapes and forms. It can be something as simple as a discount that is offered to regular customers. My editor tells me that her local bookstore routinely gives her a 10 per cent discount on book purchases. I visit a number of restaurants on a regular basis where every time I get the bill the owners have taken 10 per cent off the price. I always insist that it isn't necessary, but deep down I like it. One particular restaurateur told me that because my wife and I eat at his restaurant every week and we tell lots of our friends about how good the food is, a 10 per cent discount is cheap advertising for him.

All businesses can benefit from rewarding customers for being loyal. The hard part is to determine how you can best reward your particular customers. If there is any doubt, talk to your customers and staff. Sit down with a few people and have a brainstorming session that will identify ways to reward loyal customers. Being taken for granted is a common reason for customers changing where they shop.

42 Be one step ahead of your customers

Have you ever been into a business where they seem to read your mind? Just as you have a thought, there is someone standing beside you with the exact item that you were thinking about. Or as you stand looking at shelf upon shelf of products, a knight in shining armour comes to your rescue and hands you the exact product that you need, with a smile on his face and a twinkle in his eye.

These businesses are excellent but, unfortunately, they are few and far between. If a family enters a restaurant with small children, there is every chance that they will need a little assistance, but time after time I see families struggling to get seated and they have to ask the staff for this and that, as if they are the first family ever to dine there.

Smart customer service is all about being one step ahead of your customers—knowing them so well that you can meet their expectations without them even having to tell you what those expectations are.

Rather than waiting for the customer to make their request, try to be one step ahead of them. If they have a lot of packages, ask them if they would like them delivered or if they would like help taking them to their car. If the customer is moving house and you are the removalists, offer to give them a printed inventory of their belongings for their insurance company or to call them the day before the furniture will arrive.

If you run a clothing shop and a customer buys some clothes that will need alterations, offer to have them done before the customer asks.

Wherever possible, try to predict your customers' needs and make suggestions or recommendations that will prove useful to them.

43 Show that you are proud of your business

Being proud of your business is an admirable quality and most customers will appreciate this in any business. A business is often the result of a lot of hard work, risk, pressure and countless other emotional issues. After all of this, it seems only fair that a business owner should be proud of any achievements that they may have in their business. In fact, I think that one day a week should be dedicated to all small businesses around the world. On that day, all customers should support small businesses in their community in recognition of the role that these businesses play, often for little return. Small business owners should be thanked for doing a good job and for giving it a go.

When it comes to customer service, I have found that most of my customers are very interested in my business. When I talk to other business owners, they say the same thing about their customers. There is a degree of fascination about and admiration for small business owners. For this reason, anything that makes you proud should be shared with your customers. If you receive an award or pick up a new distributorship, tell your customers. If you employ new staff, introduce them to your customers. In fact, if just about anything happens that makes you feel proud, pass it on to your customers and they will share your pride.

I believe that customer service is a very emotive relationship. Customers enjoy feeling a part of a business and they like to be included. Having a noticeboard announcing what is happening in your business helps to bring customers into the inner sanctum.

Be proud of your business and share all of your achievements with your customers. In doing so, you will develop a relationship that will span many years.

44 Remember important dates

One of the most effective ways to make your customers feel special and important is to remember and acknowledge important dates. Your immediate thought might be dates such as birthdays and anniversaries, which are useful to remember, but there are lots of other dates that can have an even greater impact. A few suggestions include:

- The first date that a customer visited your business.
- The first date that a customer referred your business to someone else.
- The first time that a particular product was purchased.
- A milestone number of purchases.

Although it can be difficult to monitor some of these milestones, the advent of sophisticated software programs is making it easier every day. As with all monitoring, ensure that you use a system that works for you and one that can be sustained. If it is too complicated it will tend to be forgotten and fade into oblivion.

Acknowledging these dates and anniversaries can have a number of positive effects on your customers. First, it makes them feel special, which of course they are. Second, it shows that you value their business enough to monitor every purchase they make. And third, it shows that you look at the relationship as ongoing and long term.

Remembering these kinds of dates does take time and you do need to be well organised. However, relatively inexpensive computer software is readily available that can be used to organise important customer information and remind you of these special dates and anniversaries.

45 Make a visit to your business memorable

One of the great advantages that small businesses have over their large corporate cousins is the ability to form relationships with their customers. In a big firm, people come and people go, accounts are passed around the business, and when customers call they rarely speak to the same person twice. Small businesses have a much greater degree of consistency, which customers like. It's nice when you call the local butcher to place an order and he knows you, and asks about your family and your plans for the weekend. Or when a small art gallery that you have visited contacts you to tell you of a new artist's work that they think you might enjoy (and perhaps purchase).

As small business owners and operators, we should all cultivate the building and developing of these relationships. Take a few minutes to get to know your customers and always use the personal touch.

Look for little ways that you can make a visit to your business memorable. It can be something as simple as walking around and talking to your customers, perhaps giving out a few free samples or offering advice. I like to make my clients tea or coffee when they come in for an appointment. My receptionist feels that she should be the one to do this, but I enjoy making my clients a drink and I know that they appreciate it. It's a very small thing, but it's a personal touch.

The personal touch can extend to sending notes of thanks or of congratulation if a client or customer has some good fortune or a reason to celebrate. If, in the course of a general conversation, you find out that it's their birthday, shout them a product of some sort on the spot. Be spontaneous and show the customer that you value not only their business but them as a person.

Some people struggle with spontaneity, but if you work at it, you will be surprised at how good it feels and how appreciated small personal gestures are. I also believe that it is important to encourage your staff to be spontaneous.

46 Start a VIP club

Starting a club for your customers is an excellent way to maintain great service while collecting information from your customers about what you are doing well and what areas you need to keep working on.

A VIP club can take many shapes and forms, but I feel that it's particularly appropriate to any business that deals directly with the general public and has a sizeable and regular customer base. Take a hairdresser and beautician, for example. By having a VIP club, they can offer their best customers special incentives to visit the business more often. They can introduce new products and services to their VIPs at special information nights and seminars; this will not only increase sales, but will also make these customers feel that they are an active part of the organisation.

I believe that a club like this needs to be developed for the right reasons—namely, to increase the level of service offered to your customers. However, the club concept can be developed to encompass many other areas of your business and is limited only by your imagination. It's a great way to spread information, to increase awareness about your business and the products that you sell, to introduce the people working in your business, and so on.

The more effort you put into your club, the better the results will be. You may find that some of your most loyal customers will want to be actively involved in assisting with the running of your club. If they do—great. Welcome them with open arms.

47 Be patient and courteous with your customers

It can be very embarrassing for a customer to go into a business and ask for a specific product or service that they may not know much about. A smart and professional business will take the time to explain important issues regarding the proposed purchase and make the customer feel good about it and in no way inadequate because of their lack of knowledge.

There is another kind of business that seems to thrive on belittling their customers. Staff might be insensitive about correcting the customer's use of terminology. Or the customer might be treated like an idiot because they don't know the difference between a triple reverse sky sprocket and a double reverse sky sprocket. (Like, who doesn't know the difference between these two everyday items?)

Be patient with your customers, and make sure that your staff are also patient. When you do something every day, you tend to have all of the answers, but when you do it for the first time, there are a lot of logical questions to be asked. If you work with your customers and help to answer their questions or concerns as simply and as professionally as possible, they will appreciate it. This is good customer service and your business will be recognised because of it.

Never forget that no one likes to be made to feel like a fool. Keep an eye on your staff to ensure that they are always patient with your customers, and reprimand anyone who fails to display this basic courtesy. Patience is a virtue, but in a small business it's a lot more. Making a customer feel foolish is a guaranteed way of shortening the length of the relationship.

Notes

Customer Service Action List

Things to do   **Completed**

1.
2.
3.
4.
5.
6.
7.
8.
9.
10.

6 | Face-to-face customer service

This is what customer service is all about. The aim of this section is to address a number of areas that all have the same basic component—face-to-face interaction with the customer. The ideas recommended describe the sale from start to finish, from the minute the customer is welcomed into the business to the time they leave. They should be memorised by anyone who deals with customers on a daily basis.

#48   Be welcoming
#49   Be organised
#50   Be prepared to make a recommendation
#51   Talk *to* the customer, not *through* the customer
#52   Do something unexpected
#53   Remember to say 'thank you'

48 Be welcoming

A strong, warm and sincere greeting is considered one of the most basic of all customer service tips, yet it's quite a rarity these days. What is more common is either no acknowledgment or a rehearsed, insincere greeting.

You have a few short seconds to impress your customers when they first contact your business. This may be over the phone or when they are walking in through the front door. A strong and positive greeting, with good eye contact and a big smile, is the perfect way to start off the relationship.

Of course, sometimes this can be hard to do. You may have had a late night, problems at home, a difficult customer earlier that day or a host of other problems that have soured your mood. These all need to be forgotten. Every customer that walks through the door should feel important and welcome in your business.

A poor greeting is like a poor handshake—the customer goes away feeling unfulfilled.

49 Be organised

There really is nothing worse for a customer than going into a business where the staff can't seem to find anything. The simplest request is thwarted because the staff can't find a pen or the latest sales catalogue, or the credit card machine, or some other object that is essential for making a business work.

Being organised is an impressive trait that gives the customer confidence in your business. If you can't even find the simplest of items to complete the transaction, what other things could you have messed up?

Foolproof systems are great for overcoming these kinds of problems. A simple thing like attaching a pen to the counter with string to eliminate the pen shuffle is a good idea. Neat stacking of stock in the storeroom enables you to tell at a glance what you have available for sale. There are literally hundreds of ideas that you can use to improve your level of organisation and, as a result, the overall level of customer satisfaction with your business.

A constant bugbear for me is having to chase up suppliers to send me an invoice. We often have to oncharge services and we like to include a copy of the invoice to show our clients that we haven't marked it up. We can't invoice our clients until we get the bill from our supplier, so if they are slack it affects our cash flow.

If you feel that your organisational skills aren't as good as they should be, find someone who is organised and get them to help you get back on track. Often a fresh pair of eyes will pinpoint weakness in an existing system that can be easily overcome.

50 Be prepared to make a recommendation

As I have mentioned in other parts of this book, sales skills and customer service go hand in hand. Having good selling skills helps to make you better at providing customer service because your customers will leave happy.

A common trait in poorly-trained sales staff is their lack of ability, and often the confidence, to recommend a product. When I purchased my scuba diving shop many years ago, I ran into the same trap. I always felt that making a recommendation would be seen as a hard sell. It isn't. It's what the customer wants. They like to know what you would recommend. I always used to go to great lengths to tell my customers about the full range of diving equipment that my business sold, the ins and outs of each brand and product. However, the sales conversion rate was very low and I could almost see my customers becoming confused the more I talked to them.

One day a supplier was in the shop waiting to talk to me while I was serving a customer. He listened patiently while I did my full presentation and, as always, the customer walked out of the shop with a pile of brochures and a head full of information. He turned to me and said tactfully, 'You did everything except tell the customer what they should buy. That's why they left.' He sat me down and explained the importance of recommending a particular brand (his or some other company's).

At first I was a little sceptical because I didn't want to become a high-pressure salesperson, but I tried his technique on the next customer who came through the door. I explained about three sets of scuba equipment, and finally I introduced the fourth set and said, 'This is the equipment that I use'. The customer asked me why and without a moment's hesitation I said, 'Because it's the best'. Bang, I had a sale on the spot. Not only was it the best sale I had ever made, but my customer brought in five friends who all purchased a set of the same equipment. From that day on I have always made a point of making a recommendation to my customers and it has worked very well.

How many times have you been into a bookstore not really knowing what you feel like reading? You ask the sales assistant to recommend something and they mumble a few words about it being up to you. In a good bookstore, the staff will gladly make recommendations.

Don't be afraid to make recommendations to your customers. Your sales will increase and your customers will be much more satisfied. This doesn't mean that you have to become a pushy salesperson, but you have to become a *good* salesperson—that's the difference.

51 Talk *to* the customer, not *through* the customer

It's difficult not to be repetitive when you are dealing with customers all day long, especially when they tend to ask the same questions every time. Unfortunately, this is a part of our working life. We all face a degree of repetitiveness that simply cannot be avoided. But it's a shame to see people serving customers and reciting the same lines over and over, with no real recognition of the customer as an individual.

We have all been into shops where the staff appear to be bored senseless. They answer customer enquiries like a robot, barely acknowledging the customer and often simply pointing. To the customer this is almost like saying, 'You're not important. I don't want to be here and you are only adding to the boredom of my job.' I even see this happening at the end of the sale, when there is often an insincere 'Thank you' or, even worse, 'Have a nice day'.

When dealing with customers it's very important to stop for a second, make clear eye contact to acknowledge the person, and then answer their questions clearly and concisely. Don't treat them like a number; treat them like the person they are.

I often hear business owners and staff complaining about how difficult their customers are. They are demanding and rude, and they want everything done immediately. From my experience they are only receiving what they give out. Those customer service-oriented people who know how to smile and how to make eye contact establish an instant rapport with their customers that blossoms into a warm and friendly encounter, even if it's only for a few minutes. The customer leaves feeling good, and the person who was serving them also feels good and ready to start the next encounter on a bright and very positive note.

As a business owner or manager it is up to you to set the example when it comes to treating customers as individuals. If your staff see you leading by example, they will follow. If staff boredom is a problem, develop ways to overcome it. You might consider moving staff around so that they don't end up doing the same job all the time, changing the environment so that there are new and interesting things to talk about, or rewarding staff for making the effort to talk to customers—whatever works for your business. Try to keep some innovation in the workplace that will keep your staff talking to your customers.

Another complaint that I hear a lot is that the business is too busy to take the time to be friendly to customers. I still can't believe that I hear this, but I do. When things are busy, it's even more important to take a few seconds to be friendly and to recognise the fact that the person standing in front of your cash register is paying the bills. People can deal with waiting in line if they are finally served by a friendly, interested person.

The most important point to remember from this tip is that you need to be sincere when dealing with customers. If you are going to ask a question, make sure that you acknowledge their answer.

52 Do something unexpected

Exceeding your customers' expectations is often really quite easy. I was purchasing a chocolate bar recently, looking for an afternoon energy boost. It was only about $1.50 and I took it to the counter. The man serving me asked if I was planning on eating the bar today and I said I would be devouring it the minute I left the shop. He suggested that I buy the same bar that was on special in a discount box that was half price because it was almost out of date. As I was going to eat it straight away, it made no difference to me. To make the deal even better, he said that if I wasn't completely satisfied with the discounted bar he would give me the original one for free. How could I go wrong?

All of this service and recommendation happened over a $1.50 chocolate bar. I go back to this shop on a regular basis simply because of the service that I received and didn't expect to receive.

I visited a bottle shop recently to buy some wine and beer for a dinner party. There was a new brand of beer on the market that I had seen advertised that looked good and it was being sold at a good introductory price, but I thought that I would play it safe and buy the usual product. The salesman started up a conversation and I told him my concerns. He immediately offered me one of the new beers to try, which I did. I ended up buying a carton. This bottle shop is out of my way, it's not necessarily the cheapest and it's a pain to park, but I always go back because of the service that I get.

If the salesman isn't too busy, he even carries my purchases out to the car. This is out of the ordinary and, in my eyes, very good service. While I feel special as a customer, I notice that he treats all of his customers in a similar manner. This is a very successful bottle shop that thrives with no advertising.

Good customer service is all about details and doing the small, unexpected things. If you remember back to the beginning of this book, I mentioned that the key to successful customer service is to meet, and where possible exceed, your customers' expectations. Look for ways to do the little, unexpected things to make your business stand out from the crowd when it comes to customer service. People will talk about the extra little things that you do and word will spread that your business is better than the rest.

53 Remember to say 'thank you'

At the beginning of this section I explained the importance of a strong and confident greeting when meeting customers. The same principle applies to the farewell, but with one main difference. When a customer leaves your business after making a purchase, it's nice to say, 'Goodbye. Hope to see you again soon', but it's also very important to thank the person for their business.

Consumers have choices and they know that they can decide where to spend their money. Like any conscious decision, it's good to feel that you have made the right one. Assuming that everything else goes smoothly in the transaction stage of a sale, all of the benefits can be lost in the closing stage.

It drives me crazy when I make a purchase and the person behind the counter doesn't even say 'Thank you', let alone 'Goodbye'. They have moved on to the next customer and you have basically been dismissed. At this moment you know exactly where you stand in the importance scale to the person behind the cash register—nowhere.

My advice is simple: stop for a second, look the customer in the eye, thank them for their business and say 'Goodbye'. The 'thank you' needs to be sincere and focused, not just a throwaway line delivered while studying your fingernails and wondering what to have for lunch. I now stand at the counter and wait until I get a 'thank you', and on many occasions I have had to tell the shop assistant what I'm waiting for. Of course they look at me as if I'm deranged, and often they don't understand what the big deal is.

Poor service encourages more poor service. It is a cycle that makes people lose their enthusiasm for being friendly and trying that little bit harder. We have all been to a supermarket, where we tend to expect fairly ordinary service, only to be greeted by a bright and bubbly, young and enthusiastic checkout attendant who greets us sincerely, processes our goods, perhaps even engages in a little light conversation, thanks us for our business and wishes us all the best for the rest of the day. We leave these encounters feeling great. The same effort and energy needs to go into each sale and each face-to-face encounter, but it can't be forced and it has to be sincere.

A friend of mine purchased two paintings at an exhibition marking the opening of a small commercial gallery. The gallery owners not only sent her a card thanking her for purchasing the paintings, they also delivered them to her home, along with a bottle of champagne, and helped her to hang them.

Always remember to thank your customers for their business. If you find that your staff are forgetting to do this, pick them up on it immediately and don't let it become a bad habit. The same principle applies to telephone orders, Internet orders, wherever the business comes from—say 'thank you' and mean it.

Notes

Customer Service Action List

Things to do   **Completed**

1.

2.

3.

4.

5.

6.

7.

8.

9.

10.

7 | Telephone customer service

We are all communicating more on the telephone than ever before. Even with the advent of email, the telephone is still the quickest and most convenient way to talk to someone and it will likely continue to play a major role in virtually every business. Good telephone customer service needs to be resurrected. Customers expect and often demand it. For a business to meet and exceed customer expectations on the telephone, there are a number of steps that need to be clearly understood and practised. They need to become the norm rather than the exception when the telephone is being used.

#54   Ensure your automated answering service is user-friendly
#55   Answer the phone with a positive attitude
#56   Speak clearly, ask questions and give useful answers
#57   Change recorded messages frequently
#58   Keep background noise to a minimum
#59   Ensure that messages are passed on
#60   Eliminate the need for callers to have to repeat themselves
#61   Keep a pen and paper by every phone

54 Ensure your automated answering service is user-friendly

To say that I despise the new trend of automated answering services is an understatement, but I would like to make a distinction between those that work well and those that don't. If the system is easy to navigate and logical, then I have no problem with it. I do a lot of my banking over the phone: it's readily accessible 24 hours a day, it's very easy to use, and the more familiar I become with the system's features the more I use them. I would much rather use telephone or Internet banking than stand in line for half an hour waiting to see a teller.

The automated systems that bug me are those that aren't logical, where the options are confusing or don't seem relevant to my query, where it's difficult to hear, or where, if you make a mistake, you basically have to hang up and start all over again. While I don't consider myself to be a rocket scientist, I am reasonably intelligent and more than capable of following directions. Yet some automated systems simply defy all logic.

There is no doubt that automated systems have their place in our modern business world and that they are here to stay. However, if your business uses, or is planning to use, one of these systems, make sure that it is independently reviewed before you start using it and get some of your customers to trial it. The end user will always be the person that will pick up problems faster than the techno communications company that sets up the system. Probably one of the most common faults with automated systems is the use of terminology that may be very familiar to people in the business but is double-dutch to their customers.

During a recent meeting with a legal firm client, we were discussing the introduction of an on-hold system that could be used to promote the business while clients were waiting to talk to the relevant person. We decided to be unconventional and record lots of jokes about lawyers. Now, this tongue-in-cheek promotion says a lot about the legal firm. It shows that they have personality and confidence, that they are not afraid of laughing at themselves and at their profession. There is no doubt that they will stand out from the crowd and be remembered by anyone lucky enough to call them and to get put on hold.

55 Answer the phone with a positive attitude

Before picking up the telephone, stop and take a breath, smile, and then focus on the call that you are about to take. When you answer, the caller will pick up on your positive attitude and your smile, and they will automatically be more receptive to what you say.

People will always comment on a positive telephone manner, simply because it's so refreshing. This also sends the message that the business is fresh and alert and that they take an enquiry seriously.

We can all recite countless times when we have spoken to businesses on the telephone and the person answering the call sounds bored, completely uninterested or even quite rude. These calls only last a few seconds if I am making them.

The telephone is an essential tool for most businesses. But the telephone itself is the same piece of equipment for all of us. The difference is how it is used. There is no excuse for a poor telephone manner, and anyone who answers a telephone in your business should constantly be encouraged to follow the three-step principle of *stop, smile and think* before picking up the phone.

Customer service is all about attitude. To really impress your customers, you need to have the right attitude.

56 Speak clearly, ask questions and give useful answers

We have all had the experience of calling a business that just can't seem to answer any of our questions. You ring the business with a simple request, but no matter how hard you try to get an answer, it just can't seem to escape the lips of the person on the end of the phone.

Most businesses will be asked similar questions time and time again. A good idea is to keep a list by the phone of answers to the most commonly asked questions. If the enquiry can't be answered using this list, there should be details of who can answer the question and the customer should either be put through to that person or told that they will be called back within a few minutes.

A big part of this customer satisfaction tip is the importance of listening and asking the customer a few simple questions. They may not be sure exactly what they want to know, but that is why they are contacting the business. Be patient and you can normally figure out what they need, and the enquiry can then be handled quickly and professionally.

A pet gripe of mine is when the person answering the call only half listens to you, then mutters something about putting you through to someone to whom you have to repeat the whole story, only to be told that you have been put through to the wrong person and you will have to be put back through to the receptionist to have your call transferred again. I normally use my fingers at this stage to press the disconnect button and look for the next business offering the same service or product.

57 Change recorded messages frequently

If you use recorded messages, try to change them frequently. Use the recorded answering system as a marketing tool. Inform your customers that their call is important and that you would like the opportunity to respond as quickly as possible. Dull or boring recorded messages can give the impression that your business is dull and boring and, more importantly, that you are not interested in your customers.

There is an excellent service available called 'message on hold'. This provides a system where you can have a long recorded message that is played to your customers when they are put on hold. It's a great opportunity to explain various aspects of your business and how you value the business that your customers provide. These services are a relatively inexpensive way to inform your customers about:

- the types of services your company offers;
- any awards or important announcements that will enhance the image of your business;
- suggestions for ways to improve the speed with which you can process your customers' enquiries (such as visiting the website);
- your company's commitment to customer service;
- your welcoming suggestions that the customer may have that could be used to improve the overall level of service offered by the business;
- any special offers that are current;
- any jobs that may be available; and
- any operations changes that may affect customers.

The list goes on. The effectiveness of these systems is lost if the message stays the same for ten years. It should be changed on a regular basis.

58 Keep background noise to a minimum

There is nothing worse than calling a business and being unable to hear the person on the other end because of all the background noise. While it can be difficult to provide a quiet place to take calls, especially in some smaller businesses such as workshops and factories, there are always things that can be done to reduce the level of background noise. Some suggestions include:

- Partition off a part of the office to ensure that noise is dampened and less direct.
- Don't put items such as water coolers near the telephones, as people will congregate around these facilities. A group of people standing by the reception desk having a chat can be very distracting for a receptionist.
- Talk to the providers of your telephone system to find out if there are products available that can reduce or eliminate background noise.
- Some noises are more distracting than others. Music can be particularly distracting, so it should be kept at a low volume.
- Traffic flow can be distracting. Unfortunately, the nature of reception areas is such that this is where people come and go. This can often be noisy and distracting for the receptionist. Something as simple as thicker carpet around the reception area can help to make the area quieter.

Use whatever means you can to reduce the amount of noise in and around any area where people are required to answer telephones. Your customers don't want to shout to be heard, and they certainly don't want to have to repeat themselves over and over again.

Customer service encourages making every aspect of communication with your business easy and enjoyable. Customers aren't impressed if they have to yell to be heard.

59 Ensure that messages are passed on

A common complaint from customers is that their phone messages aren't passed on. This can be very frustrating and it shows a lack of communication within a business. Typically, a customer may ring with a query and the message will be passed on to the relevant person. After a period of time the customer rings again to chase up the query, only to be told that no one has received the message and the whole process has to start again.

Information needs to flow freely throughout a business. If telephone messages aren't getting through, find out why. Your customers will soon go elsewhere if a simple task such as passing on a message cannot be completed. What does it say about your business?

Information flows through many departments in larger companies and often there can be problems with one particular department. By talking to your customers and tracking down the problem area, you can usually make a few simple operational changes that will solve the problem.

60 Eliminate the need for callers to have to repeat themselves

The next time you find yourself on the telephone having to repeat the same request for the fifth time to a different person, think about how frustrating it is. Look long and hard at your own business to see if you could be guilty of doing the same thing to your customers.

One example that springs to mind for me is when I ring my credit card company to check on my account balance. The first thing the recorded message asks me for is my card number. Then I have to choose a particular option. When the call is routed to the next department, I have to punch in my card number again and choose another option. Finally, after a long wait, my call is answered by a person whose first question is, 'What is your card number?' You must be joking. This is one of the largest companies in the world, and even they can't get it right.

61 Keep a pen and paper by every phone

While this may seem obvious, it's surprising how many times you have to wait for someone to find a pen and some paper before they can take your message. This suggests to the customer that the business isn't organised and that the customer will just have to wait. How reassuring is it for a prospective customer if a business sends the message that the customer's time isn't important?

Every telephone in a business should have a notepad and pen beside it, and it should be one person's job to ensure that they are always there. If you have an office filled with pen thieves (which I am guilty of), you may need to attach the pens to the phones. At one stage, my staff tied the pens to bricks by the phones to stop me making off with them. This broke my habit and eliminated the constant search for pens around the phones. Keep message pads by the telephone, not scraps of paper. Message pads enable a record of the message to be kept so that if the original is lost there is always a back-up copy available.

When taking messages over the phone, ensure that the details are correct, the names are spelled properly and the telephone numbers are clearly written. All messages should be dated and include the time the call was received. Most important of all, the messages should be legible. A message that can't be read is potentially a lost sale.

The ability to take messages quickly and efficiently is of primary importance in the field of customer service.

Notes

Customer Service Action List

Things to do	Completed
1.	
2.	
3.	
4.	
5.	
6.	
7.	
8.	
9.	
10.	

8 | Promotional material

How does promotional material figure in the realms of customer service? I believe that it is an important cog in the entire wheel. Your promotional material needs to be well written, easy to understand, logical and professionally produced. While it is unlikely that a customer would sit down and look at a brochure and comment on the customer-friendly aspect of the business (although, hopefully, they will), subconsciously they will form an opinion of your business. The more customer-friendly your promotional material is, the greater the chance that this subconscious opinion will be a good one.

This section will help your business to produce more customer-friendly promotional material.

#62   Plan your promotional material from the customers' point of view
#63   Answer the most commonly asked questions
#64   Avoid using technical jargon
#65   Make it professional—inspire confidence
#66   Make your contact details easy to find and easy to read
#67   Keep text to a minimum—stick to the facts

62 Plan your promotional material from the customers' point of view

A key to successful promotional material is to produce it with the customer in mind. They will be the ones who will need to be convinced that your products are what they are looking for.

I recommend to our firm's clients that when they are developing their promotional material, they involve a number of current customers as well as potential customers in the process. Ask for their comments on issues such as the appeal of the material, the layout of the information, the wording of the text, the images used, the pricing, and any other information that could be relevant. I have found that people are more than willing to give their comments and opinions when asked, and the end result will be promotional material that is far more effective and better suited to your customers' needs.

All too often, promotional material is developed in the bowels of a business, with the first customer contact being when 10 000 copies have been printed. The way a business perceives itself and its products is often completely different from the way a customer perceives the same business. By trying to look professional, is your business giving the impression that it is expensive? Do the images used send the wrong message?

Where possible, involve other people in the process of designing any promotional material so as to increase its customer-friendliness. Your business will benefit from material that is far more effective, and your customers will subconsciously find your business more appealing and customer-oriented. This principle applies to all promotional material produced, including brochures, television and radio commercials, printed advertisements and websites.

63 Answer the most commonly asked questions

Whenever I am planning promotional material for my clients, I start by writing down exactly what it is they are trying to achieve. I then write down the headings *Who*, *What*, *When*, *How* and *Why*. Finally, I set about answering each of the questions as if they were being asked by a customer. The end result is the key information that needs to be put into any promotional material. A lot of material is full of long, flowing sentences filled with descriptive prose that, while pleasant enough to read, doesn't answer all of the questions that a customer may have about the product.

If a customer can read through your promotional material and gather just about all of the information they need, your material has worked. The next step is to get the customer to buy the product, and if the material is right, this should only be a formality. If they have read your material and there are a lot of questions to be answered, it can often end up in the 'to do later' pile or, worse still, in the 'too hard' wastebasket.

Remember that customer service focuses primarily on making the sales process easy and uncomplicated for your customers. Well-thought-out promotional material is a big step in the right direction.

64 Avoid using technical jargon

We live in an age where new words are being invented by the minute. Technical jargon is commonplace in many industries, and at times it's almost like learning a new language. Not a day would go by when I don't hear some new term and have to stop and ask someone what it means. It is also the age of the acronym, where new words are developed from the initial letters of a group of words. In fact, there are now dictionaries to help us to understand this developing new language.

Many very experienced advertising people suggest that any promotional material or advertisement should be written so that it can be understood by a nine-year-old. Right or wrong, the principle is spot on. Keep it simple and avoid using technical jargon and buzz words.

By saying this, I don't mean to imply that most customers are stupid. As you will know from reading this book, that is an issue that I am very passionate about. It simply means that we should all try to make our promotional material as easy as possible to understand. By all means include the technical jargon if it's appropriate to your industry and relevant to the specific piece of promotional material being designed, but avoid it like the plague for mainstream information.

Technical jargon has its place, but strong, simple language will always prove more beneficial in the long run. Your customers will understand it completely and there will be little room for misinterpretation or confusion.

65 Make it professional—inspire confidence

Your customers will form a lot of opinions about your business simply by looking at your promotional material. For this reason, it's important to send them the right messages. It's important for it to look professional. All of the other tips included in this section look at other aspects of your promotional material which are important, but if you don't inspire confidence in your business capabilities with smart, professional promotional material, the rest is a waste of time.

I often see businesses trying to cut corners with their promotional material simply to save a few dollars. They print it in one colour instead of four because it will save 20 per cent on the cost. This is a false economy. The whole aim of promotional material of any kind is to attract more customers. It needs to look impressive. A potential customer needs to read it and say to themselves, 'Yes, I would buy from this business'.

Don't scrimp when it comes to presenting your company. Spend a few dollars and develop well-designed and well-written material that you will be proud of. Don't print brochures on flimsy paper—buy quality paper. Get a good laser printer in your office to make your documents look the best they can. Print up envelopes—they cost the same as buying them plain off the shelf. Do all of the things that will give your business a strong corporate image and that will inspire confidence in it.

Another point to remember here is that the use of scantily clad models to sell spanners is really inappropriate. Yes, sex sells, but we are in a slightly more sophisticated age than we were in the 1970s, where buxom young blondes were used to sell everything from fried chicken to socket sets. Use beautiful people in your promotional material by all means, but avoid being sexist. Opt for professionalism every time.

66 Make your contact details easy to find and easy to read

Always put your contact details in a logical location, in bold type that is easy to read and easy to understand. It can be very frustrating when you are reading a brochure and it's nearly impossible to find the contact details for the company that produced it. Surely, getting a customer to call is the entire reason for producing the promotional material in the first place.

I have an older friend whose eyesight is starting to fade. He constantly complains that he can't read the text in a lot of brochures and advertisements. If you are targeting an older clientele, remember this point and make the text easy to read.

Nowadays there are many ways to contact a person: faxes, telephones, mobile phones, pagers, letters, emails and probably a few more, such as the carrier pigeon that may make a strong recovery one day. If you have access to all of these gizmos, make sure that your customers know about them and which one is the best for them to use to contact you.

Another important item to include in your promotional material, especially if your customers will visit your place of work, is what hours your business is open. For the sake of good customer service, the easier you make it for your customers to contact or visit your business, the more satisfied they will be with the overall experience.

67 Keep text to a minimum—stick to the facts

When it comes to promotional material of any kind, I always recommend that text be kept to a minimum. Stick to the facts. Quality copywriters will always tell you that the less you write, the more you sell—and I agree.

Many people try to include as much text as possible in their promotional material. All you need to do is answer all of the necessary questions (see Tip #55) and present the information in a simple, clear and easy-to-read manner. If a brochure contains too much text, it simply gets thrown away.

Whenever you are producing promotional material, look for ways to reduce the amount of text and leave some open space. Use short, sharp sentences that set out the facts clearly. Sell the benefits to the client of using your products and services and leave it at that. Repeating yourself over and over shows a lack of confidence in your products.

I strongly suggest that you get as many people as possible to read your promotional material before going to print, and that you assess all of their comments. Your natural impulse may be to include more information, but if you are brave enough to use the 'less is more' principle you will find that your promotional material will work far more effectively and your customers will notice that it is very customer-friendly. Everyone wins, which is one of the objectives of customer service.

Notes

Customer Service Action List

Things to do   **Completed**

1.

2.

3.

4.

5.

6.

7.

8.

9.

10.

9 | Customer service and the Internet

The Internet is here to stay. Many businesses have embraced it, many are considering embracing it and some think that it's a waste of time. I believe that the Internet is one of the best customer service tools any business can have. It provides access to information that your customers can use at their convenience, a very significant advantage when considering the customer service value of the Internet. Like all aspects of customer service, there are some common mistakes made. This section looks at ways to ensure that your business takes full advantage of the Internet, using it to increase the overall level of customer service and, ultimately, the level of customer satisfaction.

#68   Make your website user-friendly
#69   Use your website to answer questions
#70   Respond to emails quickly
#71   Don't 'shout' or use abbreviations
#72   Use photos of real people
#73   Make automated responses simple and professional
#74   Keep text on websites to a minimum
#75   Ask your customers to review and rate your website
#76   Update your website regularly
#77   Beware of spam

68 Make your website user-friendly

I have mentioned throughout this book that customer service is about meeting and exceeding your customers' expectations. The Internet can feature significantly in this area. Unfortunately, websites are still in their early stages of development and even if they look very impressive it doesn't necessarily mean that they are good. Considerable resources are committed to the appearance of a website, making sure that there are lots of bells and whistles. Most of the time, these are completely unnecessary. Customers are going to a website for information. In some instances they will make a purchase, but it will generally be driven by the information that is provided on the site.

I cannot emphasise enough the importance of having a simple, easy to use and informative website. When thinking about the layout of your site, make sure that you ask as many people as possible for their ideas and input. Check out as many websites as you can to look for ideas and inspiration.

Another common problem area with websites is that an IT wizard checks it out, rather than a potential customer. Before you launch your website, test it by finding twenty people who would be the kind of people that you would want to attract to the site and see what they think about it. Is it easy to navigate through, is it fast enough, is it logical, is it easy to read and, most importantly, would *you* use it?

I recently came across a website selling products to an elderly market. The text was so small that I could hardly read it; I can only imagine what it would have been like for someone who is a bit older and with failing eyesight.

Make your website as easy to use as possible and be open to input from the customers who will ultimately be using it.

69 Use your website to answer questions

Whenever I am developing a website for a client, I sit down and work out what messages we want the site to get across. There are questions that will need to be answered, so I make this a priority. I write down all of the questions that could be asked and then I set about answering them, making certain that *Who*, *What*, *When*, *How* and *Why* questions are all answered.

Once I have done this, I classify the questions into groups and categories and then work on the layout. The use of pictures and flashy graphics comes into play at the very end of the development project. These are really the wrapping that makes the site more visually stimulating, and in some instances they provide a great way to see a product.

Continually update your website to ensure that the questions that you are answering are still relevant. Add new questions and answers as your products develop.

Good customer service on the Internet is about looking for ways to pass on the information that the customer is looking for, as quickly and easily as possible.

70 Respond to emails quickly

Research has shown that the number one reason businesses fail to succeed when selling products online is that they take too long to respond to an enquiry. It's hard to believe, but true. Why go to the trouble and expense of building an impressive website that is focused entirely around instant, 24 hours a day, seven days a week access, and then blow it all by taking a week to respond to an email enquiry?

The Internet is an instant access facility that, ideally, will save us all a lot of time. As customers, we have grown accustomed to the instant access that the Internet provides, so having to wait for a response is incredibly frustrating.

Recently a friend had a problem with his Internet Service Provider, so he emailed them. He received a response saying that they were inundated at present and it would take them eight days to get to the problem. My friend couldn't believe it. How appalling is that for customer service? This was a very large company, which reinforces my belief that people will start to move away from these organisations because they cannot provide the same levels of service that smaller companies can.

If your business does receive enquiries over the Internet, make sure that someone is ready to respond promptly. People understand time differences. They realise that if they have contacted you from New York and your business is based in Australia, there will be a slight delay before you can respond, but you should definitely be able to get back in touch within 24 hours at the latest.

I feel that this is a particularly important point for after-sales service. Most companies respond quickly when there is the possibility of an order, but they move a lot slower when it's a follow-up question or request for information. Both should be treated as equally important.

71 Don't 'shout' or use abbreviations

'Shouting' in email terms is when you use capital letters in your correspondence. We all receive emails that are full of capitals urging us to respond immediately. LAST CHANCE, ONE AND ONLY OPPORTUNITY, etc. It's designed to catch your eye and make you respond quickly. The same principle applies to those people who indicate that every email they send is urgent. Both of these antics tend to irritate people who treat them as urgent and needing attention, only to find that they are direct sales pitches.

The use of abbreviations in an email is equally frustrating, especially if you have no idea what the abbreviations mean. Corresponding by email is quicker than writing a letter or sending a fax, but the same rules of etiquette apply. All emails should be correctly addressed, names should be spelled correctly, and the body of the message should be well written and proofread carefully. If it isn't urgent, don't mark it as urgent.

As time goes on we will all utilise email more and more as a fast, efficient and cost-effective way to communicate, but when it comes to offering good levels of customer service, be careful of being overly casual and informal when contacting people, especially if you don't know them very well.

72 Use photos of real people

A large part of customer service is the concept of developing long-term relationships. While the Internet can enable a small business to look like a large business, it is somewhat impersonal. The use of photos of key people in your organisation will help to bring people inside your business and give them more of a personal feel about you. This is the beginning of a customer relationship.

I don't really understand why more businesses don't put photos of people on their websites, but I'm certain that this will change over time. Research shows that advertisements featuring people in media such as the Yellow Pages, newspapers and magazines tend to have much higher success rates than those that don't use them. I believe that the same principle applies to websites.

If your customers will be dealing with a particular person, put their photo on the site so that they can form a mental picture of their contact within your organisation. Show them photos of your business, where it is located, what the office or workshop looks like, even a few photos of your city and the key attractions in the region.

Another great way to develop a relationship is to include a photo of a happy customer along with a written testimonial about your products or services. If you include photos of people and places on your website, your customers will be more inclined to use your business because they can see who they are dealing with.

73 Make automated responses simple and professional

One aspect of the Internet that can be a real trap for your customers is that it can be a very impersonal form of communication. One way to overcome this, to a degree, is to utilise automated responses on your website. This means that whenever someone contacts you or places an order, an automated message is sent to them, thanking the customer for their business and advising them of the status of their order.

Amazon.com are very big advocates of this form of customer service. Whenever you make a purchase from this company you will receive an email confirming that the order was received, a confirmation number and an approximate shipping date. You are then advised of when the package has been shipped and the approximate arrival date. The next email that comes through thanks you for making a purchase from Amazon.com.

While all of the above is fully automated, you can't help but be impressed by both the accuracy and timing of the follow-up. Someone has put a lot of thought into the after-sales contact for this company.

Automated responses can be used in a variety of situations, but they all work the same way. When a customer carries out a particular action on your site, they will receive a follow-up email, sent out at a time determined by you.

74 Keep text on websites to a minimum

Forcing your customers to wade through page after page of information isn't good customer service. Think about your website from your customers' point of view. What information are they likely to be looking for, and what is the best format to use to give it to them?

I often see websites that have been produced with the text from the company brochure simply converted and put on the site. I believe that you should rewrite any information that you plan to put on a website. The Internet is a different medium and it has far more scope than a brochure. There are links to other areas, interactive components (press this button and something will happen) and the potential to be updated regularly.

Because of this flexibility and potential, you should look long and hard at what information you put on your website. Generally, though, I believe that it's important to keep written text to a minimum. Long pages of text are hard to read on computer screens. It's far easier on the eyes to have smaller amounts of information spread across more pages. Some Internet developers maintain that you should never have to scroll down when using a website. All of the information relevant to that particular section should fit into one screen.

Of course, there are exceptions to this. Some sites are purely information services where customers will expect to have to toil through page after page of information. How nice and unexpected it is when you go to a site and find that it's surprisingly easy to use.

I believe that text should be written specifically for your website and that it should be kept to a minimum. Give people the facts in a professional, easy to read and easy to navigate manner. Put the flashy graphics at the end.

75 Ask your customers to review and rate your website

I recently developed a new website to promote my books and other services offered by my company (www.AndrewGriffiths. com.au). When the site was first designed, I emailed the web address (URL) to over 500 of my friends and clients for their opinions, feedback and suggestions for improvements. The response was great, with most people replying within a few days.

Some simply said that the site was excellent and they really liked it; others went through it with a fine-tooth comb, picking up some spelling mistakes and a few links that didn't work as well as they should. Some others gave great advice on what they thought the site needed to make it more customer friendly.

All in all, within a day or so, I had received an abundance of information from my customers and friends about my website. These suggestions definitely improved the site, and there were a number of ideas put forward about aspects of the site that I had overlooked.

People like to be asked their opinion. They will give you their ideas and views freely. Sometimes their ideas and suggestions will be good and sometimes they will be shockers, but whatever the suggestion, take them all on board. If you are uncertain about a particular recommendation, ask a few other people for their opinion. Smart, successful people are never afraid to ask the opinions of others about any aspect of their business.

When developing a website, remember that the end user will determine whether or not it works. This makes it a very logical step to ask a few customers for their thoughts on anything your business does but, in particular, on your Internet presence.

76 Update your website regularly

As the Internet is still in a relatively new stage of development, technology is changing daily, along with the style and look of websites generally. I often speak to businesses that are fed up with the Internet. They tried a site and it didn't work, so now they have decided that the whole Internet thing is a waste of time. Believe me, it's not. I have a number of clients who have built exceptional businesses based entirely on the Internet. These businesses understand that making a business work online takes persistence and a commitment to improving and updating their website on a regular basis.

If you have the kind of site that you would like people to come back to on a regular basis, you need to change it regularly to make it more interesting and look for ways to catch the visitor's eye. Many changes to a site can be automated to allow for different photos and text to come up each time a person visits your site. Talk to your website developer about what you are trying to achieve with your site and go from there. They should be able to offer a number of options to suit your budget.

If you are serious about developing an online aspect of your business, you should budget for ongoing costs associated with updating your website on a regular basis. Your customers will notice the changes and they will be impressed. It will encourage them to keep coming back to the site and, best of all, they will subconsciously classify your business as a good provider of customer service.

77 Beware of spam

Spam is electronic junk mail. Of course, it isn't necessarily junk, but it *is* unsolicited information sent to a prospective customer. Some businesses have embraced spam with a passion. I'm sure that we all receive some form of junk mail several times a day. Very often we don't even take the time to read it; we simply press 'delete' and it's gone.

The Internet makes it easy to send a pile of information to a large number of people, very quickly and inexpensively. This doesn't mean that you should go overboard when sending electronic mailings. Using the Internet to advise potential customers about your products is fine, but don't start stalking them. A better option is to offer a free newsletter of some sort, which visitors to the site can subscribe to. They will then be expecting your emails and it will seem less invasive.

The main problem with inundating potential customers with emails is that they can ultimately start to resent your business. It is like a pesky telemarketer who won't take 'no' for an answer.

A couple of other key areas that can really upset receivers of spam are marking it as urgent when it isn't, and attaching a large file that takes forever to download.

Spam is a powerful marketing tool, but remember the principles of customer service. It is easy to press a few buttons and to be anonymous, but for every email that is sent, there is a real person sitting at a computer somewhere in the world who will have to open and read your message. What message do you want them to have about your company?

I also believe that it is a good idea to have your company's policy regarding spam included on your site. Here is an example:

Spam policy
The Marketing Professionals are aware of their corporate responsibilities as good Internet citizens and are dedicated

to protecting the privacy and rights of other Internet citizens. We are strongly opposed to the sending of unsolicited email (spam) and have made every effort within our power to discourage and prohibit the sending of spam.

We are highly sensitive to the privacy of each of our subscribers and will not make their name, address, or any other information that they have provided us available to anyone without the subscriber's express permission.

Our definition of spam

Spam is any unsolicited email. This includes any promotion, information or solicitation that is sent to an individual without prior communication between companies requesting information.

What is not spam

An email message is not spam if the recipient in anyway requested email be sent to them. Sometimes bulk emails may be sent to clients to update them on various topical issues. These bulk mailings will always have an easy option to allow the recipient to be removed from the mailing list. Our aim is always to ensure that you are informed but not inundated.

The main aim of making a statement like this is to show your customers that you respect their time and their privacy. This is an important aspect of customer service.

Notes

Customer Service Action List

Things to do	Completed
1.	
2.	
3.	
4.	
5.	
6.	
7.	
8.	
9.	
10.	

10 | Following up on a sale is good customer service

Many people think that a sale ends when the customer walks out the door. For some smaller-priced items, it does. I wouldn't expect my local convenience store to make a follow-up call to check if I was satisfied with my purchase of a carton of milk. But for higher-priced items and services, following up after a sale is a surefire way to ensure that your customers are very satisfied with your level of service. Even if the customer isn't happy, at least you have the chance to do something about it. This section highlights the importance of following up on a sale and suggests a few ways of going about it.

#78   Discuss the sale on the spot
#79   Make a follow-up call
#80   Explain what to do if there are any problems
#81   Contact customers that you may have lost

78 Discuss the sale on the spot

Some businesses make a point of talking to their customers about their service on the spot, while it's fresh in the customer's mind. This is a good practice to follow, as over time people's perceptions change.

Several years ago, I flew from Chicago to London. I had travelled with British Airways from Australia and I was half-way through my trip. While waiting in line to check my bags through, I was approached by a customer service representative who asked me if I would mind answering a few questions about how I had found dealing with British Airways. As I was standing in a queue and not going anywhere for a few minutes, I was more than willing to assist. I explained that my experiences with the airline had been very good, with only a few minor hiccups that we all expect from time to time with any international travel, such as delayed departures.

The man interviewing me was very polite, and he asked me some excellent questions which showed that the company was looking at all levels of service. I was most impressed, and after arriving home I received a thank you letter with a complimentary upgrade certificate that I could use the next time I flew with British Airways. This experience reinforced for me the value of asking customers on the spot about their experiences.

When asking customers about their degree of satisfaction with a product or service, always remember that they may be in a hurry, so explain who you are, what you would like and how long it will take. I also think that, where possible, it's a nice gesture to give them something to thank them for their time. It doesn't have to be much, just a small token of your appreciation.

Our company recently conducted a major market research campaign at a busy international airport. We had to survey 1000 departing tourists about their experiences and their degree of satisfaction with a particular holiday destination.

Most people were more than happy to discuss the good and bad things about their holiday; most importantly, it was fresh in their minds. To thank them, we gave everyone a high-quality postcard which they could fill in and post from the airport.

I sometimes visit a cafe that is close to my home, because the coffee is good and it's on the water, so the view is nice. The service is shocking, though—the staff just can't get it right. I would love the owner to come up to me one day and ask me what I think. I know that the business could increase its sales by at least 30 per cent with some simple operational and customer service changes and I would gladly tell them how to go about it, but I don't think they are interested.

Take the time to ask your customers their thoughts on your business, right there on the spot.

79 Make a follow-up call

I am a strong believer in making follow-up calls and I recommend this to most of my clients. Follow-up calls give the customer the opportunity to say their piece, whether it be good or bad. From my experience, most people are forthcoming and usually have positive or constructive things to say.

Think back to the last time you visited your dentist. Did you get a follow-up call a few days later to make sure that everything was OK and that you were happy with the service that you received? Probably not.

I could rattle off a hundred examples of businesses that could really benefit from making follow-up calls, but I am sure that if you were to think about it for a few seconds, you would quickly determine whether your business fits into this category or not.

I recently started doing work for a telecommunications company and the first call to action that I suggested was the implementation of three follow-up calls to every new customer. The first call was to be made the day the customer's paperwork was received, the second when the customer was connected (about a week later) and the third a month later to make certain that everything was OK. The response was overwhelming, to say the least, especially at a time when telecommunications companies are not renowned for their levels of service.

Making a follow-up call is an obvious thing to do, but few businesses do it. Making a quick call to ensure that your customers are happy could easily be the best money your business can spend.

Some time ago I had my car serviced. I was a bit shocked by the bill, but after a few days I received a follow-up call from the mechanic, just to make sure that everything was OK. I said that I was surprised by the amount of the bill, but otherwise I was happy. He suggested that we run through it to make sure that no mistakes had been made, and within a few minutes I was completely satisfied with the bill and all of the costs incurred.

But just to make the experience even better, he offered me a free wash and detail the next time I had my car serviced. This guy was good—very good. I would probably not have gone back to his garage because I wasn't happy with the bill, but after a few minutes on the phone, my entire perception had changed and now I take my car back there all the time.

Consultants rarely make follow-up calls to see if the client is happy with the work completed. Solicitors, accountants and other professionals, likewise, rarely pick up the phone to determine your degree of satisfaction with the work they have done.

Imagine buying some new clothes and having the fashion store phone you a few days later to make sure that you are happy with your purchases! Even if a customer isn't happy, by making a follow-up call you now have the opportunity to rectify the situation and, most importantly, keep them coming back to you.

Making a follow-up call is an impressive form of customer service. Its simplicity is wonderful and the long-term benefits are astounding. I have yet to come across a business that couldn't benefit from making follow-up calls.

80 Explain what to do if there are any problems

A concern that customers commonly have when making a significant purchase is what will happen if there is a problem with the product after the sale. To eliminate this concern, I suggest that you develop the habit of explaining exactly what the customer should do if there is a problem.

I recently went to my doctor who prescribed some medicine for me. She warned me that, in a very few cases, the medicine could have some side effects. She then explained exactly what they could be and what I should do about them if they occurred. I was instantly reassured and felt very comfortable knowing that, while I might experience a few side effects, I knew exactly what to do and if I was uncertain or concerned in any way, I was to call my doctor immediately.

Associating doctors with customer service may seem somewhat unusual, but this doctor is a natural at customer service. She managed to make the entire experience easy for me and made certain that if I encountered any problems I would have a course of action to follow to sort them out.

This same principle can be applied to many other situations. If there is any possibility, no matter how remote, of something going wrong with your product, let your customers know in advance how you will handle it. After-sales service is becoming more of an issue in today's consumer-based world. I am sure that many people reading this book will have observed that customers ask about after-sales service far more today than they did in the past.

There are advocates out there who will say that by talking about possible problems after a sale, you may lose the customer. From my own experience, I would say that the opposite is true. Not talking about possible problems and what to do if they arise leaves the customer wondering what will happen if there is a problem.

Have confidence in your products and in your after-sales customer service. This confidence will be picked up on by your customers, and the perceived risks associated with making a purchase will be reduced. As a final point, if you are going to offer excellent after-sales customer service, make sure that you mean it and that you can deliver it. Remember that how your business handles problems will have a major impact on your customers' perception of your business and on their willingness to tell their family and friends about you.

81 Contact customers that you may have lost

For a lot of businesses, staying in contact with customers is somewhat awkward, especially if considerable time has elapsed. Often customers that are no longer visiting your business are simply classified as lost.

The reality is that there could be a simple reason why the customer hasn't been in for a while. Whatever the reason, it's good for you to know, especially if the customer was with you for a long time.

It only takes a few minutes to make a quick telephone call or to drop a past customer a quick letter to say hello. There is nothing at all wrong with mentioning that you haven't seen them for a while and you were wondering if everything was OK with the products that you sell or the services that you offer. You may find that there was a problem that you can rectify easily over the telephone in a few seconds. It may be that a competitor has opened up that is better located or better suited to meet the customer's needs. It may be a simple financial matter. Whatever the reason, you need to know.

I have seen a lot of businesses dig out their old customer files and start doing a bit of a ring around, and all of a sudden they have attracted a pile of new business, simply because they have called at the right time.

Other business owners have found that their accounts department has continually been messing up the invoicing, to the point where the customer has simply had enough. You may find that if you have reduced your profile in the business, your customers aren't as happy to deal with your staff—they started using your business because of you, and if you aren't the one that they deal with now, they may decide to go elsewhere.

Contacting 'lost' customers is an interesting exercise, to say the least. It may be a little confronting for some people, but for those that are serious about customer service it's a very good exercise that will pay for itself many times over. Remember, also, that people love to hear from the boss or the owner of a company.

Notes

Customer Service Action List

Things to do   **Completed**

1. ----
2. ----   ----
3. ----   ----
4. ----   ----
5. ----   ----
6. ----   ----
7. ----   ----
8. ----   ----
9. ----   ----
10. ----   ----

11 | Internal customer service

Customer service is often considered an area of a business that concerns only sales staff or showroom staff. This can cause a lot of problems, and generally the customer is the one that suffers and ultimately leaves, never to return. Every person within an organisation needs to be committed to offering high levels of customer service. This section will look at identifying areas that can cause problems, the end result of these internal problems and what can be done to overcome them. This is an excellent section for department managers and people in charge of larger organisations.

#82   Work closely with other departments
#83   Don't let the customer suffer because of
         internal bickering
#84   Follow up on calls from people within your organisation
#85   Give your customers a contact number for outside
         normal hours
#86   Don't keep your customers waiting on hold—offer to call
         them back

82 Work closely with other departments

If you own or manage a large business, this customer satisfaction tip may be applicable to your business. Sometimes larger organisations have interdepartmental communication problems that can affect customer service.

Cooperating with other departments can sometimes be a strain. I recommend that the entire customer service process be applied to the behind-the-scenes aspect of your business. Survey all departments to find out what problems they may be experiencing when it comes to carrying out their normal day-to-day activities. Are there particular problem departments that cause delays? Are there ways to improve communications and speed up the process of doing business?

Develop an internal marketing campaign that encourages each department to work together for the benefit of the business's customers. There really is no excuse for different departments not working together, but sometimes these situations just evolve.

If your customers deal with different departments in your business, ask them if they have problems with any specific department. Identifying these problem areas is an important first step in resolving them and moving towards better levels of service, both internally and directly to your customers.

83 Don't let the customer suffer because of internal bickering

Some businesses seem to struggle to process simple orders. This can be a source of constant aggravation for customers. Delays can be experienced, paperwork can be lost, mistakes can be made with paperwork and orders can be despatched incorrectly. Sometimes there can be petty grievances between departments. Perhaps the accounts department doesn't get on with the sales department, so processing of bills is given a low priority.

If you have identified that there may be an internal problem between departments, it needs to be sorted out quickly and with a minimum of fuss. The main aim of any business is to ensure that the customer is served promptly and efficiently and that any bickering between departments is kept away from the customer.

The last thing a customer wants to hear from the salesperson is how hopeless the despatch department is and that their order will likely be filled incorrectly. Dirty laundry needs to be kept internal. Sometimes blaming another department is an easy way to hide a mistake made by a member of staff. It's easier to say that the order is wrong because someone in the factory made a mistake than to admit the order was taken incorrectly in the first place.

All that the customer expects is that their order or request for products or services is processed quickly and efficiently. If this simple task cannot be accomplished, all of the other customer service tips discussed in this book won't be of any use.

84 Follow up on calls from people within your organisation

I have discussed the importance of following up on calls from customers—it's absolutely essential if you are to have any degree of customer satisfaction, let alone a profitable business. The same principle applies internally in a business. Some departments are notorious for not returning calls. When internal calls are received, they seem to be given a low priority, with the excuse given that the person was too busy.

Customer service has to be developed within an organisation. Departments need to be made aware of the important role that they all play, and of the ramifications of not offering good service to other departments.

One of the best ways to get a feel for this is to spend time in other departments, seeing what happens when a customer's order isn't delivered correctly because of a simple typographical error or when a customer is lost due to a poor customer complaint resolution department.

The real issue here is to convince staff within an organisation that every other department is a customer and they should be treated accordingly. One of the simplest ways to get this started is to implement a time limit for all calls to be answered. Make it realistic, but enforce it. All interdepartment calls have to be answered within two hours, say. If a call isn't returned, there needs to be a good reason. While this may be seen as a tough form of action, it ensures that communication is speeded up. If a customer then calls you with an enquiry that you need to follow up with another department, you will be able to do so confidently.

85 Give your customers a contact number for outside normal hours

It can be very annoying to have to call a business that closes at 5 p.m. on the dot and opens not a minute before 9 a.m. If you need any form of customer service outside of these hours, forget it.

For many businesses there is probably little need for customers to call outside of normal hours, but for others there may be a lot to be gained from making themselves more available to their customers. What if something goes wrong with the product? What if there is a breakdown? What if someone doesn't turn up at the agreed time? Often customer service is about planning for the worst: what to do when things turn ugly. If you have a contact number that your customers never have to use, great. But if they have a number that they can call in an emergency, and they have to use it, that is giving them good customer service.

There are a couple of points to remember with emergency contact numbers. The customer should understand how to use the number, otherwise it may become their main point of contact. If you are the person who has to answer the phone, this can become a little frustrating. Outline clearly to your customers when the number should be used and in what kind of situations.

If you are going to give someone an emergency number to use for outside of normal hours, make sure that someone is going to answer it. It's no good having the direct telephone number for the President of the United States only to hear when you call it as some disaster threatens, 'Hi, this is the President. I'm not here right now, but leave your name and number and I'll get back to you before the next election.' A tad silly perhaps, but I'm sure you know what I mean. Don't just give out a number in anticipation that it will never be called. Plan for the fact that the number you give out *will* be called.

This leads to my third point: you need to decide what level

of service you want to offer. I couldn't think of anything worse than being on call 24 hours a day, seven days a week, but it's unlikely that there would be a marketing crisis that needed to be handled after hours. I do, however, do a lot of public relations work and some of my clients could find themselves in need of public relations advice after hours. In these cases, they have my after hours contact details should an emergency arise.

If you give out an after hours contact number, don't sound irritated when your customers use it. Recently I was on holiday in a fishing port and I picked up a brochure that offered full-day fishing trips. As I had arrived late in the evening, I thought it would be too late to book a trip for the next day. However, the brochure included a 24-hour booking number, which I rang, only to be lectured on how rude I was to ring at that time of night. I asked the woman why she promoted a 24-hour booking service if she didn't want to offer one, and she had a few more choice words to say. I hung up and booked another boat the next day.

86 Don't keep your customers waiting on hold—offer to call them back

Getting through to some businesses can be challenging, to say the least. If your customers are phoning with a specific enquiry that may take more than a few minutes for you to deal with, offer to call them back rather than making them wait on hold.

I have done a lot of research on customer service and, without doubt, when it comes to the most common complaints, failing to return telephone calls is up there near the top of the list. So, if you offer good customer service by telling your customers that you don't want to keep them waiting on hold, make sure that you follow through and call them back quickly.

I know what it can be like when things get busy around the workplace. It's easy to get sidetracked and diverted from your mission and your responsibility to your customer, but if you say that you will call them back, make sure that you do. If the customer's request is going to take longer than you first anticipated, give them a call and let them know that you are working on it and that you should have an answer by a certain time. Think back to those times when you have waited for a call back from a supplier, only to have to chase them up time and time again. Are you likely to want to deal with them again in the future?

Notes

Customer Service Action List

Things to do   **Completed**

1.
2.
3.
4.
5.
6.
7.
8.
9.
10.

12 | Maintaining a personal commitment to customer service

Customer service starts at the top and works its way through an entire organisation. It takes a real commitment from everyone involved to make it work and often it can be hard to maintain the momentum. This section offers suggestions for ways to keep the momentum and commitment firmly at the front of everyone's mind.

#87   Write a mission statement for customer service

#88   Be consistent in all you do

#89   Read books and magazines to look for ideas

#90   Look at other successful businesses for ideas

#91   Don't discuss politics

#92   Know when to take a break

87 Write a mission statement for customer service

Writing a mission statement that outlines what your business thinks about customer service is an important step in the overall commitment to customer service. A mission statement is a powerful document that puts your thoughts, goals and objectives into a kind of balance. For some reason, writing down these thoughts makes them more real.

A customer service mission statement is something that all employees should be familiar with. It should be put on the wall in a place where everyone can see it—staff, customers and suppliers alike. If you do this, you will be amazed at the comments that you will receive from these people.

A customer service mission statement only needs to be about a paragraph long. Here is our company's statement:

> As a team of dedicated professionals our aim is always to treat our customers with the respect that they deserve. We acknowledge that they have chosen to give their business to us because they believe in us, a trust that we will always honour. We are committed to exceeding our customers' expectations and to delivering the highest quality of work possible. We will work with our customers and we will build long relationships that will span many years. We will grow through referrals from clients who have become firm believers in our commitment to customer service.

Take a few minutes and write your own customer service mission statement. Both you and your customers will benefit from it.

88 Be consistent in all you do

One of the greatest ways to ensure that your customers are really satisfied is to be consistent in all aspects of your business. Offer consistently good levels of service, open at the same time consistently, sell the same products consistently, have the same faces behind the counter consistently. Consistency is a powerful tool that all customers like and feel secure with.

Restaurants and cafes that can offer consistently good meals and service are almost guaranteed to succeed. Unfortunately, many offer consistently poor meals and lousy service.

Working towards a level of consistency is harder than it sounds. People, by their very nature, tend to change things around. That is the nature of the universe. For this reason, offering a consistent product or service is tough. It's the principle that the fast-food giant McDonald's has been built upon: consistent hamburgers and fries anywhere in the world.

Customers look for consistency in businesses. If you can meet this expectation, you are well and truly on your way to really impressing your customers.

89 Read books and magazines to look for ideas

There are many sources of inspiration when it comes to looking for new ways to offer better levels of customer service. There are some excellent business magazines and books that deal with the subject of customer service. I have recommended a few at the back of this book.

I also enjoy reading magazines from various industries that have articles on customer service. They can provide great ideas that can be used in any business, even if they are not normally associated with your particular industry.

Most newspapers have business sections, and often these have articles covering new and innovative customer service suggestions. It is an area of business that is growing more important every day. As the products and services offered by businesses become more similar and prices become closer, customer service is the one thing that will set two similar businesses apart.

To be committed to customer service, you need to accept that it is an ongoing project. You don't just get up one day and find that your level of customer service is perfect, enabling you to forget all about it. You need to develop a real interest in the subject and look everywhere for new ideas that you can use in your own business.

The more committed you become to customer service, the more your staff will start to share your enthusiasm. Your customers will notice and they will talk to their friends, and your business will grow as word of mouth starts to spread.

90 Look at other successful businesses for ideas

We have all heard the term 'mentor'. This is where you find a person whom you admire and they take on the role of an adviser. They share their experiences freely and help you to develop your own skills and style for running a business or working in a job.

This idea is similar. You find a business that you really admire and you build your business following their principles of success. Once you have become committed to offering quality service, your eyes begin to open and you really start to notice service in all of its good and bad forms. For example, you might go into a hotel restroom and notice how clean it is. The wastepaper baskets are empty, the soap dispensers are full, it smells nice, there is plenty of toilet paper and the whole area is sparkling clean. In the past, you might not have noticed if it was clean or dirty.

You might start to notice interactions between staff and customers that previously you would have paid little or no attention to. Each time you make one of these observations, try to remember it or jot it down on a pad. Write down the good and the bad. Learn from them all. This exercise will make it easier for you to be objective in your own business. You might recognise that some of the areas where you previously thought you offered pretty good customer service could be improved.

By becoming more observant of other businesses, you will soon pick up countless ideas that could easily be implemented in your business. Equally as valuable, you will see many of the mistakes commonly made by businesses. Observing these at first hand makes them much easier to avoid yourself.

91 Don't discuss politics

Have you ever walked into a business and started talking to the person behind the counter, only to be bombarded with a pile of opinions about fairly personal issues? Some people insist on giving their views on everything, to everyone, and this can easily offend.

While I encourage sincere conversation with customers, it's important not to cross the line. How do you know what their political or religious views are? I remember waiting in a queue at a petrol station once while the attendant was busy telling a customer a joke about a gay man. The station was full of people and no one laughed when the punch line was delivered. It was inappropriate, and the poor fool behind the counter didn't even realise his error of judgment after the event.

There are a number of issues that I feel shouldn't be discussed in a customer service situation. The main ones are:

- religion;
- politics;
- sexuality;
- personal details; and
- race issues.

It's important to train your staff to avoid discussing these topics and to be aware of them yourself. Inappropriate discussions can cost customers. Stick with safe topics that still enable you to have an opinion but which are unlikely to cause any insult to your customers.

92 Know when to take a break

From time to time we all need a break. For a lot of business operators, it's difficult to find the time, the money and the staff to replace you when you do take a break. The end result can often be that holidays aren't taken, and over time stress and tension build up to the point where the level of customer service starts to suffer.

We all need to be able to recognise when we need a break. There are many telltale signals indicating that your stress levels are building. They include:

- You are abnormally irritable. Situations that you would normally handle easily become mountains, and you find that you are losing your temper more on a regular basis.
- You are constantly fatigued. Being tired is a very common symptom of stress. Typically, no matter how much sleep you get, it's never enough.
- You generally feel unwell. If you find that you are having difficulty fighting off colds and other common ailments, you may be run-down, another common symptom of stress. Frequent headaches also seem to accompany increased levels of stress.
- You lack the ability to concentrate. This shows that you are not functioning at your best as a result of stress.

There are, of course, many other signs and symptoms that can indicate that you are suffering from a stress build-up. The most important thing is to do something about it.

I always recommend regular check-ups with a doctor. If you are concerned that your stress levels are really high and you are starting to feel out of control, don't be embarrassed; simply visit your doctor and tell him or her exactly how you are feeling. If you don't do something about it, things will only get worse and the stress will manifest itself in more startling ways each time you ignore it.

The hardest part of dealing with stress is trying to figure out what you can do to relieve it. Everyone is different. I know that for my wife, shopping and general pampering are great stress relievers. I prefer a nature fix—camping, fishing, a walk in the rainforest, or something else that ensures that I am well away from telephones and computers.

Identifying what works for you is an important step in overcoming the ravages that stress can bring into your life. To work at your best level, try to find what works for you and do it as often as possible. Take holidays regularly. Even if you can't afford the ideal, round-the-world, first-class type of holiday, at least take a few weeks off just to stay at home and enjoy some time out. Exercise, catch up with friends, read some good books, or just watch a pile of videos and play with the dog for a few hours every day.

Just as it is important for you to recognise when *you* need a break, you must be able to identify when your staff need a break. Keep a close eye on everyone you work with and look for the telltale signs of stress creeping into the workplace. If you feel that someone is starting to show signs of stress, talk to them and give them an opportunity to explain how they are feeling. Suggest that they talk to their doctor. This is a delicate situation that requires sensitivity.

I have worked with some pretty serious characters in the commercial diving field and the gold exploration industry. These were hard men who aren't the stereotypical stress sufferers, but believe me, there were plenty of teary people over the years who simply let stress take control of their lives. I also have battled with stress over the years.

Don't underestimate the effects of stress on you and your staff. The end result can be lost customers and permanent ill health.

Notes

Customer Service Action List

Things to do   **Completed**

1.

2.

3.

4.

5.

6.

7.

8.

9.

10.

13 | When things go wrong

Let's be honest—every business has to face the occasional customer complaint. For some people this is a real challenge and it can be very disturbing and confronting. This section looks at the various kinds of complaints that businesses may receive, and it offers suggestions for handling them correctly and, hopefully, retaining the customer. While it is important to have a very clear policy in place, it's just as important to look at each customer complaint on an individual basis.

93 Have a clear and concise policy, but be flexible
94 Dealing with telephone complaints
95 Dealing with written complaints
96 Dealing with a third party complaint
97 Always have a solution
98 You just can't please some people
99 The importance of following up a complaint
#100 Get it right the first time
#101 Make one person responsible for monitoring customer service

93 Have a clear and concise policy, but be flexible

Every business needs to have a clear plan for what to do when it receives a complaint. Some people feel that putting this kind of plan in place is an admission of some sort of business failing, but it's quite the opposite. By having a simple, easy-to-implement plan that can be actioned whenever a customer has a complaint, you are simply acknowledging the fact that we are all human, and that sometimes mistakes happen. If you get a complaint from a customer, don't torture yourself about it; move forward to resolve the complaint and keep the customer as happy as possible.

A customer complaint policy should be a simple document that covers the following:

- How staff should act when taking a complaint from a customer. This includes acknowledging the complaint, listening to the customer and letting them air their grievance, ways to handle an angry or threatening customer, and some simple techniques for dealing with confrontation of this nature.
- Establish exactly how the customer would like to see the complaint resolved.
- Determine who should be involved in the complaint process. Is the complaint fairly simple to resolve on the spot, or should other, more senior members of staff be involved?
- Record information about the complaint. If the complaint cannot be resolved on the spot, what information needs to be recorded to ensure prompt processing and resolution?
- Advise the customer of what steps will be taken to resolve their complaint and the expected time frame for the resolution process.
- Advise the customer who will be handling the complaint and give them their contact details.
- Ensure that the complaint is followed up and that the customer is satisfied with the outcome.

Once you have developed your customer complaint policy, make sure that all of your staff read and fully understand it. They may have suggestions for improving the policy and their comments should be taken into consideration. All new staff should be trained to know and understand all aspects of the customer complaint policy, and this training procedure needs to be repeated on a regular basis.

Now that I have said that you should develop a complaints policy, please don't become completely inflexible, hiding behind the policy as a convenient barrier. We all hate hearing the words, 'That's our policy and we can't make exceptions'. Good customer service is all about ensuring that your customers are satisfied with the service that you offer. Look at each individual complaint from the customer's point of view and aim to resolve it in a fair manner. If this falls outside of the policy, so be it.

Complaints are a by-product of having customers. As long as you deal with them promptly and professionally, there is a good chance that you will keep your customers and they will become even more loyal simply because you handled the situation well. There is a blank customer complaint policy form at the back of this book that can be adapted for use in your business.

94 Dealing with telephone complaints

Telephone complaints can be distressing, especially if the customer is particularly angry or emotional. Like any complaint, it's important to follow a very straightforward plan that is aimed at resolving the conflict.

With telephone complaints, I suggest the following:

- Make sure that you have a notepad handy and write down all of the relevant details.
- Let the customer talk. It's important that they are allowed to explain their complaint fully. Don't interrupt unless you would like clarification of some aspect of the complaint.
- Write down their name, and the date and time of their call.
- Empathise with the customer without admitting fault. Make comments such as 'I can see how frustrating that must have been' or 'It sounds like you have had a bad experience'.
- If they are being abusive or using bad language, you are entitled to ask them to refrain from swearing. The best approach to take is to assure them that you want to help them, you understand their frustration, but swearing or becoming angry won't help the situation.
- Ask the customer how they would like to see the situation resolved.
- Advise them of the course of action that will be taken by the company. Assure them that their complaint has been lodged. Make sure that they are given specific details as to when they will be contacted and by whom.
- If you cannot deal with the complaint, pass it on to the relevant person and ensure that they are given all of the details, as well as the expectations the customer has for the complaint to be resolved.
- Follow up on the complaint with the person who is handling it.

- If appropriate, contact the customer after the situation has been resolved to ensure that they are satisfied.

These are all steps that can go a long way to resolving a customer complaint quickly and efficiently, and with a little luck and good management you may even be able to keep the customer.

When a customer makes a complaint, we should all be grateful because it gives us the opportunity to rectify a part of our business that may not be up to scratch. Unfortunately, most customers don't complain—they simply go elsewhere and are lost forever.

95 Dealing with written complaints

If someone has taken the time to sit down and write a letter of complaint, it's a fair bet that they are very unhappy. If I have reason to complain to a business, I always put it in writing. Sadly, the majority of letters that I have written over the years have simply gone unanswered, which of course makes the complaint even worse.

I wrote to a restaurant once where our meal was a disaster from start to finish. The food was fine, but everything else just fell apart. The restaurant was in a large hotel, so I addressed my letter to the general manager. He rang me as soon as he got the letter to let me know that he would look into it. He was very professional, apologetic and considerate. He asked for all of the details and I was impressed with his approach to handling the complaint.

Within a few days I had received a letter back from him, unreservedly apologising about the incident and inviting my entire party back to the restaurant for a complimentary meal. We took him up on the offer, went back and had a great time. Now we are regulars and we have been for several years.

This was a very professionally handled complaint. The general manager was smart, and because he handled it so well he not only retained some good customers, he also managed to get us to tell others about the restaurant.

I have had other business owners ring me and abuse me when I have sent them letters. How dare I write to them complaining about my experience and the lack of service? I had one chap screaming at me down the phone. Imagine how much business he has received from me since.

In the same way that if you receive terrible service or have a bad experience you should take the time to write a letter of complaint to the business owner or manager, it is also a good practice to write and offer praise when you receive excellent service. Both are great forms of feedback, and it's up to the relevant people to take advantage of them.

96 Dealing with a third party complaint

If you hear from a third party about a complaint to do with your business, you can still act on it and try to resolve the situation. For example, you might bump into a friend in the street. While chatting with your friend, he mentions a particular shoe shop and you immediately start to tell him about a bad experience you had with the shop. Unbeknown to you, your friend is a good friend of the person who owns the shoe shop and he goes back and tells them the story you told him. If this business owner is like most people, he will simply throw imaginary darts at you for complaining. However, if he is really smart, he would give you a call or drop you a letter saying that he had heard about your experience and would like a chance to rectify your complaint.

Who does this? No one. Why? Because it's easier not to confront the situation. We all hear complaints on a day-to-day basis from friends, family members and associates. It's quite rare that complaints about our own business get back to us via the grapevine, but if they do, it's a fabulous opportunity to take control of the situation and to try and win back the customer.

97 Always have a solution

The aim of any complaint is to have it resolved. If a solution cannot be found, then both the person making the complaint and the business receiving the complaint lose out. Whenever someone makes a complaint, ask them how they would like to see it resolved.

Of course, the customer's ideas on how to resolve it won't necessarily agree with the business owner's, but whatever the outcome, it does need to be fair. I have had a number of complaints against businesses that have cost me a lot of money. In one instance I had to pay over $18 000 because of a company's negligence. They offered me $2000 in compensation. This was, of course, ridiculous; what was worse, it was insulting. Finally they agreed to cover their mistakes and to pay the full amount, but by now the relationship was destroyed and there was no way we could ever do business together again. We both lost in this situation: even though I received full compensation, I lost a good business relationship.

We all need to enter a complaint situation willing to resolve it. If the company you are complaining to is completely at fault, they will normally fix the situation quickly. There is no point in letting it drag on. If the fault is harder to determine, things can start to get messy. In some instances, it may be best to call in a professional mediator to try and resolve the complaint. This person is impartial: their job is to look objectively at the entire situation and find the fairest resolution to the problem.

Like all of the tips in this section, the best solution is that the customer is satisfied with the outcome of the complaint and everyone moves on with their lives. Hopefully the customer will be impressed enough with your complaint resolution skills to keep using your business.

98 You just can't please some people

We all encounter the occasional customer whom we simply cannot please, no matter how hard we try. These individuals can be soul destroying. I have had a couple of clients like this and, for whatever reason, the relationships were always strained. I never enjoyed any of the work I did for them and I spent countless hours lying awake in bed at night wondering what to do about it.

One day it dawned on me that the best thing I could do was to be honest and tell the clients how I felt, which I did. I also told them that while I appreciated their business, I felt that I couldn't give them the service or the products they needed and I gave them a list of other companies that I suggested they deal with.

I found this incredibly empowering. Instead of dreading doing work for these organisations, we simply parted company. It wasn't personal; it was just a decision that was made for all the parties involved. The 99 per cent of my clients that I have had wonderful relationships with over many years give me confidence that the work performed by my company is of a very high standard. But it is a simple fact that you can't keep all of the people happy all of the time.

I believe that customer service is a lot about honesty and openness with the people who do business with your organisation. Sometimes things won't work out, which is OK. Move on, but move on nicely. Don't mess difficult customers around simply because you don't like dealing with them.

Great customer service is knowing how to sack a customer and still be friends afterwards—a truly elusive goal.

99 The importance of following up a complaint

The biggest complaint about complaints is a lack of follow-up. If a customer goes to the trouble of making a complaint, either in person, over the telephone or in writing, the very worst thing that you can do is to ignore it. This only adds insult to injury.

A friend of mine recently complained to a sales assistant that she had received change for a $20 note when she had handed over $50. The manager was called and he spent some time checking the till against the cash receipts tape. My friend was required to wait around while this was done.

The manager finally said that he would have to wait until close of business to check if there had been a mistake. He asked for a phone number to contact her, and she is still waiting for the call. This business has opened only recently and one wonders how long it will last if its customers' complaints are handled in this manner. The manager lost a perfect opportunity to secure a loyal customer by showing concern for my friend's predicament and handling her complaint quickly and courteously.

A lot of the time, customer complaints aren't handled or processed properly simply because no one knows what to do. Often they are put at the bottom of the in-tray because people don't like to deal with conflict. In some cases it may mean that someone will lose their job, and if you are the person processing the complaint, others may blame you for it.

Whatever the reason, customer complaints cannot be ignored. Ensure that the right systems are in place so that complaints cannot be covered up or hidden in the system. Make it mandatory that any complaint received by your business should be brought to your attention.

When training your staff, emphasise the importance of handling complaints professionally and promptly. I once received a response a year after I had written a letter of complaint to a department. It's hard to believe that my complaint had been shuffled from desk to desk for all that time before someone finally wrote to me to apologise. While it made me a little angry, I have to admit that I was impressed that my complaint hadn't just been thrown in the bin.

100 Get it right the first time

Every business, whatever its size, will have to deal with customer complaints at some stage. You may find yourself having to deal with customers who are difficult and demanding. They may have a complaint that you feel isn't justified, or you may be 100 per cent in the wrong. Whatever the case, there is a right way and a wrong way to deal with customer complaints.

If you handle the complaint well, the end result may be that you appease the customer and they are satisfied with how their complaint is dealt with, resulting in them remaining a customer of yours. If you handle it poorly, they will never come back again and they will tell their friends not to use your business. The only real loser in this situation is you.

The real dollar value of losing customers due to poor handling of a complaint can be quite amazing. If I spend $10 a day on coffee from a local coffee shop, that makes me worth about $3650 a year to that particular business. Multiply that over a few years and the real cost of losing a customer soon becomes apparent.

The moral to the story is that the best way to handle customer complaints is to avoid having them arise in the first place. Make sure that you have the systems in place and the ongoing monitoring to reduce the chances of customer complaints. Most importantly, stay in touch with your customers, ask them about your business, and make certain that they are completely happy with the service that you are offering.

101 Make one person responsible for monitoring customer service

This tip really could appear in any of the sections in this book. It is an important piece of advice and so I thought that making it Tip #101 would give it special emphasis.

Making one individual responsible for monitoring your business's customer service has a number of benefits. These include the following:

1. Customer service is monitored continually, not just when time permits.
2. Customer complaints end up on one desk and this means that any disturbing trends, such as numerous complaints about one particular staff member, become obvious immediately.
3. When customers contact the business with a customer service issue, everyone in the business knows whom they should be talking to.
4. Positive changes are just as likely to be noticed by this person and they can pass this feedback to all other staff and management.
5. Your customers will be impressed by the fact that there is a specific person allocated to the task of monitoring and maintaining levels of customer service.

I am not saying that you need to employ one person full time to manage your customer service (although it would be nice), but rather that you are making one person in your business responsible for managing and monitoring all aspects of your customer service.

One way to illustrate this point is with the use of marketing. A number of my small business clients struggle to market themselves. They rarely commit time and resources to marketing simply because they are busy doing what they do to make a living. Everyone is responsible for doing a little bit of the marketing but the end result is that it rarely gets done. When one person in the business is given the responsibility of carrying out marketing, it always gets done much more effectively.

An important consideration when making one person responsible for managing your customer service is to make sure that all other members of your team realise the importance of this role. Even though this individual is managing customer service, everyone else plays an integral part in making certain that your business delivers high levels of customer service in an effort to satisfy your customers.

So whether it is making certain that customer complaints are followed up, that customer satisfaction surveys are conducted periodically and customer service audits done on a regular basis, or any of the other suggestions made in this book, making one person your customer service manager will have many benefits—the most important being increasing your chances of keeping your customers happy with your business.

Notes

Customer Service Action List

Things to do   **Completed**

1. _____   _____

2. _____   _____

3. _____   _____

4. _____   _____

5. _____   _____

6. _____   _____

7. _____   _____

8. _____   _____

9. _____   _____

10. _____   _____

Bonus section—20 more customer service tips

This bonus section looks at a further twenty customer service-oriented tips that can have a big impact on your business. They are some of my favourites, and while they can seem surprisingly simple, I can assure you that they are very powerful.

#102   Be aware of cultural differences
#103   Always think about your customers
#104   Visit your customers' businesses
#105   Embrace new technologies
#106   Invite good customers to special, exclusive events
#107   Keep databases accurate
#108   Package so as to be remembered
#109   The little things make the difference
#110   If you go to the customer's home, clean up after yourself
#111   Run an outrageous promotion
#112   100 per cent satisfaction—guaranteed
#113   Avoid being overly familiar with customers
#114   Avoid the biggest mistake—not delivering on time
#115   Go shopping at the competition
#116   Set up a customer hotline
#117   Simplify your paperwork
#118   Using reply paid mail
#119   Start a local campaign encouraging customer service
#120   Introduce a free service
#121   Don't let customer service stop when you are busy

102 Be aware of cultural differences

I live in a tourist town on the edge of the Great Barrier Reef, so I am fortunate to have a lot of interaction with people from other nationalities. The city of Cairns has over two million tourists a year, both from within Australia and from around the world. International tourists, in particular, have different customs and cultures, and it's very important to take notice and be aware of these differences.

Mistaking a Japanese visitor for a Chinese visitor, or vice versa, is insulting to both nationalities. Talking loudly and waving your arms in the air can be seen as threatening, as may physical contact (apart from shaking hands) or standing too close. With Koreans, deference should always be given to the oldest man in the group. This is their custom and a sign of respect. Certain religions prohibit the eating of meat—in particular, pork—so serving up a leg of baked ham to a group of Muslim visitors is probably not going to go over too well.

There are many ways to find out about cultural differences between countries. Of course, the Internet is a great source of information; however, there are also business groups and organisations that will be able to give you an insight into any cultural differences that you should be aware of.

We recently had a convention of 4000 Korean Amway salespeople in town. The group organising the event published a list of Korean customs in the local paper, and any business involved in the event was given detailed training sessions prior to the group's arrival to ensure that any cultural differences were overcome. All staff were given a small phrase book that they could use if they were asked a particular question by a Korean delegate.

The event was a major success and our city is starting to see a growth in Korean tourist arrivals as a direct result of the word-of-mouth publicity gained from 4000 very happy delegates.

A key point that is repeated throughout this book is the importance of understanding your customers and identifying their needs and expectations. By taking a little time and effort, you can achieve these results and completely satisfy your customers, even when they are from a different culture.

103 Always think about your customers

This is a key to excellent customer service. Show customers that you are thinking about them and their needs. Something that I have done for years is to cut out articles from newspapers that may be of interest to my clients. I have one client who is a leading organic dairy farmer and manufacturer. This is an innovative field and at present there is a lot of information in the news about what goes into our food. By cutting out these articles and posting them to him, he knows that I am thinking about his business and helping him to stay in touch with world developments.

My lawyer often sends me articles about copyright law and copies of advertisements that are interesting or unusual. I always appreciate receiving these and I ring him to thank him. It is excellent public relations for his firm and it costs only a few cents to do.

Recently I witnessed a charming example of this tip being put into practice. It was a very hot day and a woman arrived at a local cafe with a beautiful labrador and a small puppy. She tied them up outside, went inside to order a coffee, then came back outside and sat at a table. The waitress brought out the customer's coffee and a large bowl of water for the labrador and a small bowl of milk for the puppy. She wasn't asked to do this; she did it on her own initiative. The customer was very grateful (as were the dogs) for the waitress's thoughtfulness and I think it's fair to assume that this cafe has a new loyal customer.

Using your initiative to try and assist your customers and help them wherever possible is a state of mind. Poor customer service businesses tend to have staff who all appear to be wearing blinkers. It's virtually impossible to get their attention and you have to wait at the counter for the two staff to finish their discussion about the weekend's activities before you can be served, which is, of course, very frustrating.

There is a cafe in the highrise building where my office is located. Often we hold meetings there, or have a meal, or just a quick coffee to get out of the office. The staff are excellent. Not only do they know my name and the names of all the members of my team, but they make each coffee unique and a little bit special. In the creamy froth they make shapes such as love hearts, stars, flowers or swirls. It may sound corny, but they bring the coffees to our table and explain that the hearts are for the women in the group and the flowers for the men. This always goes down well and shows that they haven't just made us coffee like every other cafe; they have made it a little special and have thought about what they are doing.

The same business delivers your lunch when you order it, rather than keeping you waiting around. It's always well packaged and several serviettes are included, neatly folded. This business has gone from a struggling enterprise to a booming, very busy and, I would imagine, very profitable cafe in a relatively short amount of time.

Let your customers know that you are thinking about them. They will be impressed.

104 Visit your customers' businesses

If you deal with a lot of other businesses, it's really beneficial to take the time to visit them. This may not always be possible if there are geographical constraints, but how often have you been dealing with a good local customer for years, yet you have no idea what their business premises look like or what they actually do?

Take some time to drop by and see where it is that your customers spend their day. This may give you an insight into them and the way they think and work. It shows that you are taking an interest in them. This interest needs to be genuine if it is to benefit both your customer's business and your own.

105 Embrace new technologies

Technology is a remarkable tool for all businesses. Today we have incredible computers, telephone systems and office machines, and unprecedented access to information. This technological revolution is here to stay for at least the foreseeable future and with it comes the opportunity for customer service to really shine.

There are now more ways than ever before to communicate with our customers: telephones, mobile phones, facsimiles, email, the regular post and, of course, the main advertising media of radio, television and newspapers. For many people, keeping up with the rapid technological changes can be somewhat daunting. For those that do, it is liberating. The time and money that can be saved using the new technology is astounding.

I constantly promote staying in touch with your customers as a good form of customer service. Sending a short email occasionally is an excellent way of staying in touch without being invasive or overly time-consuming.

Computers and their associated software have made it a lot easier for businesses to produce quality in-house promotional material such as newsletters that enable you to stay in touch with your customers. Websites are another excellent way to disseminate information and they can serve as a 24-hour-a-day customer service representative.

It's important to note here that there is a difference between staying in touch and stalking. A number of suppliers send me a couple of emails every day—and they are graphics-intensive emails so they take a while to download and clog up my email. I don't even read them—I simply send them to the trash—but I still have to go through the process of downloading them. This isn't clever; it's overkill and it stops me wanting to use these businesses. I have continually asked these companies to stop sending me information, but they ignore my requests. This is the ultimate in bad service. If I could just get a monthly update on their products and services, I would be more inclined to use them.

Use technology to increase the level of service that you offer, but don't abuse the relationship just because it's easy to communicate.

106 Invite good customers to special, exclusive events

The large national store Country Road offers homewares, fashion and furniture. It is an upmarket chain and targeted at a specific market. A clever piece of customer service that they offer is to invite regular customers to exclusive pre- sale events. This means that their 'special' customers can have the run of the shop the night before the sale goes public. They get the best pick of the bargains that are available. It is exclusive and it makes these good customers feel special.

Many financial organisations, such as fund managers, hold lunches featuring a well-known guest speaker. They will invite their regular clients to attend the lunch, either for free or at a subsidised rate. There are many industries where this is a normal and accepted business practice, but there are many others where it isn't as accepted as it should be.

Each year in Cairns we have a large horseracing carnival. It's extremely popular, with people travelling from around the world to attend. All of the main local companies have marquees set up around the racetrack and they invite their key customers to join them on the day, with all expenses paid. The champagne flows, as does the fine food and good cheer, and the day is always very successful. Once again, it's all about being made to feel special.

As a marketing company, we book and recommend a lot of advertising on television, radio and in newspapers. The local media sponsor the launch of new movies as they come to town and invite all of their best customers to these exclusive premieres. We get free tickets to the movies once a week and we leave the cinema with a sense of gratitude for being appreciated by the media organisations that we deal with.

107 Keep databases accurate

How often do you receive a piece of junk mail with your name spelled incorrectly? Many businesses collect databases covering all of their customers. This is a great idea, but databases need to be managed. There is nothing more irritating than getting the same misspelled junk mail year after year.

A lot of companies have now really started to pour resources into their database management to ensure that the details are kept accurate and up to date. The more accurate your database is, the more beneficial the list will be.

Many small businesses have quite large databases, sometimes consisting of thousands of names. But due to a general lack of time or know-how, the list becomes dated and the business stops using it because they have lost faith in it. You need to allocate time and resources to maintaining and updating any database. If you don't want to do this, don't bother starting one.

I have seen a lot of small businesses really develop well by using their databases: hairdressing salons, restaurants, retailers, accountants, financial advisers and many more. The database can be used to keep their existing customers well informed about new products, services and special offers. As these people are already customers, you have a far greater chance of selling to them.

Customer service is about making your customers feel special. You have taken the time and the money to produce something to send them. Of course you are trying to sell it to them, but good selling skills and customer service go hand in hand. If your databases are inaccurate, you send a completely different message—that the customer isn't important enough for you to take the trouble to spell their name correctly.

Use databases to increase sales and the level of customer service that your business offers, but make sure that you keep them accurate and current.

108 Package so as to be remembered

Packaging and wrapping—the presentation of your goods—is one area where you can really make your business shine and be remembered. Good customer service has many steps, and one of the keys to success is to improve the level of service that your business offers during each step.

There was a time when many businesses really made an effort to package your purchases well. This may have been the local supermarket, where the person at the checkout counter put some thought into making certain that the bread wasn't put at the bottom of the bag with the potatoes on top of it, or the department store where your purchase was gift-wrapped. With the constant pressure to reduce costs, this level of service has almost vanished to the point where, for many companies, packaging is almost considered an irritation rather than an opportunity to provide excellent customer service.

There is also a move towards making packaging far more environmentally friendly. For this reason, it's a good idea to use recycled material where possible or even to provide packaging that can be reused by the customer. One very good example of this, which has been introduced in recent years, is the reusable envelope. You may receive your telephone account in an envelope that can be reused and sent back to the telephone company with your payment enclosed. For those businesses that send out a lot of mail, this isn't only a cost-saving mechanism (you don't need to insert a reply paid envelope), it's also an environmental statement and it encourages people to pay their bills faster.

I recommend that you review your packaging process and look for the following key points:

- Is your packaging material as good as it can be?
- Are your staff trained to package products well?
- Will the packaging that you provide protect your product for its complete journey?

- Is your packaging environmentally friendly?
- Can you make it easier for your packaging to be handled?
- Is your business promoted on your packaging?
- Are your customers happy with your packaging?
- Is your packaging staff-friendly—that is, is it easy to use?

By doing a packaging review you may identify a number of areas that could be improved and the end result will be a much higher level of customer satisfaction.

109 The little things make the difference

The little things are often the most important when it comes to customer service. I don't believe there would be too many businesses out there that couldn't do a number of little things to improve their overall level of customer service. Today, these little things are setting businesses apart. What do I mean when I talk about the little things? Here are a few examples.

When I was enjoying an early morning cup of tea in a cafe recently, the owner brought over a plate of toast which she said was on the house. I was a regular and she just wanted to thank me.

Following a delicious dinner at a new restaurant, my group were full to the brim and decided against ordering any dessert. A few minutes later the bright and bubbly waitress brought over two desserts and a bundle of spoons and said that they were on the house as a way of saying 'thank you'.

A while back I purchased a state-of-the-art fish tank filter from a pet shop. After about a year it started to play up, so I took it back to the shop. The owner said he would have a look at it and give me a call. A few hours later he actually dropped it back at my office with firm instructions on how to clean it properly (oops) and saying there would be no charge. This fabulous gesture will ensure that I keep going back.

These are just a few stories that spring to mind, but over the years there have been many more. Think about your own experiences, when someone has really gone out of their way to offer excellent service. Often it's only a small gesture, but it can have a profound effect.

Look for the small things and do them as often as you can and you will develop a reputation as a quality service provider. The word-of-mouth advertising and recommendations will attract plenty of new customers.

110 If you go to the customer's home, clean up after yourself

A lot of businesses involve visiting people's homes or workplaces. For all of us, this can be a dubious time. In the last week I have had two tradespeople visit our office. The first was checking the air-conditioning and the second installed a new telephone extension. Both parties made a mess, leaving grubby fingerprints on the walls around the areas where they were working, and they disappeared for hours at a time, leaving their tools and ladders set up in prime places such as our company boardroom. Wrong, wrong, wrong.

I now have a negative impression of both of these organisations. They both did an adequate job, but they were messy and, I feel, inconsiderate of the fact that we run a business.

I have a friend who runs a filtered water company. He installs water cooler machines at hundreds of businesses every year—everything from mechanics' workshops to hospitals. He makes a point not only of booking in a time to install the machines, but also of taking his own cleaning materials so as to ensure that the mess is kept to a minimum and is cleaned up immediately. He also visits regularly those of his customers whose business is hard on the machines. For example, he has one machine in a tyre fitter's workshop, so it gets covered in dirty marks from the staff. He pops in regularly to clean the machine so that it sparkles. His philosophy is that a dirty machine reflects more on him than on the business where it has been installed. As a result, he does very well. This is an excellent form of customer service that directly benefits him and strengthens his long-term relationship with all of his customers.

Another example of this suggestion, and one that most of us can relate to, is getting your car back from the mechanic's workshop and it's covered in oily finger marks, or there are shoeprints on the mats and a general grubbiness that perhaps wasn't there when the car was dropped off. Those workshops that are aware of this and go to great lengths to ensure that the car is cleaner when it leaves than when it arrived, shine in the area of customer service. I use a workshop now that washes and vacuums the car free of charge after every service. I know that I am paying for this service indirectly, but I believe that the customer satisfaction level is much higher than the alternative of saving a few dollars and having the car returned grubby.

One company that has developed a very good reputation in this area installs burglar alarms. The installers are all issued with mats to put on the floor before they do any work, and they have portable vacuum cleaners to thoroughly clean their work area before they leave. A few minutes' extra work makes for a much happier customer.

111 Run an outrageous promotion

Sometimes it's a good idea to run a promotion simply for its own sake, rather than to increase the amount of money coming into your business. Look at running a promotion that will encourage customers to talk about and remember your business for a long time.

Two examples of outrageous promotions that I have seen include:

A radio station management team car wash

The management team at a local radio station had to set up a car wash and detail the station's advertising clients' cars. If the clients weren't happy with the job done, the cars would have to be cleaned again. This was a fun promotion, but it was also very clever. It showed that the managers of the station didn't place themselves above their customers. It showed that they were prepared to humble themselves in order to do a good job to the complete satisfaction of their clients.

Managers become delivery people

The managers at a furniture store became the delivery people for a day. In a series of television commercials they used the promotion, 'If you buy from us today, we will personally deliver it to you tomorrow', and true to their word, they did. Were they busy? You bet.

While these types of promotions can have a positive impact on sales, they do much more than just that. They reinforce a commitment to customer service that is sometimes hard to get across in more conventional ways. It is the commitment from the top down which gives it even more value.

Various pizza restaurants have tried to do the same kind of promotion, where the meal is ready in a certain time or it's free. Once again, this shows a commitment to customer service.

Look for ways to run promotions that will spread the word that your business is all about customer service. Don't be afraid to be a little outrageous from time to time.

112 100 per cent satisfaction—guaranteed

As stated throughout this book, there are three steps in the customer satisfaction process:

1. Find out what your customers expect.
2. Meet these expectations.
3. Where possible, exceed these expectations.

If you can promote the fact that you offer 100 per cent unconditional customer satisfaction guaranteed, there really is no risk to the customer. The weakness with this offer is building the credibility with your customers that it is a bona fide offer, not just a promise containing lots of small print that will result in them never being able to claim a refund because of a technicality (such as the complaint wasn't lodged on the first day following a full moon).

If you are really going to be committed to offering complete customer satisfaction you will reap great rewards, because there is no risk to your customers and as a result they will keep coming back to your business and recommending it to their friends. But, and it is a big 'but', your offer has to be genuine and real. Customers aren't stupid and they will see through hollow promises and shallow guarantees. Treat your customers with the respect that they deserve: when you make a satisfaction guaranteed offer, don't cheapen it with hidden catches.

Use the slogan in your advertising and on your flyers and, most importantly, believe in your product enough to offer this kind of guarantee.

If you have a good customer service system in place, complaints should be minimal. Even if they do occur, they will be handled well and resolved quickly and professionally.

113 Avoid being overly familiar with customers

This problem can be hard to overcome if it is a personality trait. Some people are simply overly familiar with their customers. Relationships develop over time, not in the first few seconds of an encounter.

I visited a coffee shop near my office a while back and the woman behind the counter asked me where I worked. When I told her, she announced that she didn't like one of the women who worked in my business. She raved on for a few minutes until I stopped her, telling her politely that she was talking about my wife. I then walked out, never to return. Such a silly thing to do. She is entitled to her opinions, of course, but if she starts talking about someone from my office, there is a good chance that they are someone I like and respect.

Another example of this is those people who call you and try to sell you something. The conversation starts with no introduction other than a few questions about how your day is going. As they may be a customer you answer them court-eously, but the point to the call seems a long way off and finally, when prompted, they tell you who they are and what they are trying to sell you.

Some sales representatives are like this as well. You meet them once and then they act is if they are your best friend. Over-familiarity can vary from annoying to downright scary. Your customers should set the familiarity boundary and this should always be honoured and respected.

I used to dine at a particular restaurant on a fairly regular basis. They offered good food, at good prices, and the atmos-phere was excellent for conducting business meetings over a meal. Over time, the staff, who were normally excellent, started to become far too familiar at inappropriate times. One time, I was discussing a new project with a prospective client. There were papers all over the table and we were talking quite intensely when the head waiter came over with a glass of wine. He sat down at our table and began to complain about how bad business was. What was worse, he wouldn't leave. My prospective client was clearly perturbed by what was going on and kept looking at his watch. It was a very awkward situation. I finally had to ask the waiter to leave us as we had to talk business. He jumped up, slammed the chair into the table and stormed off in a huff. He virtually threw our meals at us and refused to acknowledge me as we left. The meeting was a disaster.

I understand that this waiter was probably only trying to be friendly, but he overstepped the boundaries in too many ways. As I was a regular, he assumed that we were becoming friends. At any other time, if I was by myself, I would gladly have had a chat. His actions during this meal, though, were completely inappropriate and I didn't go back to the restaurant for years.

I suggest that you think back to the times when you found yourself in a situation where a stranger was basically being overly familiar and how it made you feel. Then make certain that no one in your business falls into the same trap.

Monitor your staff and make sure that the boundaries aren't overstepped, particularly in a male–female encounter. There is nothing worse than a woman going into a shop and having to put up with male attendants checking her out or chatting her up. This is way out of line and absolutely no way to interact with a customer.

It's great to develop a friendly relationship with your customers, but there definitely have to be boundaries. I explain this to my staff, especially if they are young and still feeling their way in the corporate world.

Some people have a problem with the server–customer relationship. They either feel inferior or they dislike serving people. Be on the lookout for this kind of attitude, as it can do your business a lot of damage. Find people who enjoy serving and hang on to them. They are worth their weight in gold.

114 Avoid the biggest mistake—not delivering on time

This is a big issue and one that most businesses are guilty of at some time. There are a number of reasons why businesses don't deliver on time. From my experience, the following are the main offenders.

First, in an attempt to keep the customer happy, the business will promise to deliver a product or service within a certain time. They know full well that they won't be able to deliver but are afraid that they will lose the sale if they admit they can't comply with the customer's delivery time frame.

Second, a disorganised business can often have poor ordering techniques that cause longer than expected delays in providing goods and services. All orders may go through once per week, so if you miss the ordering day you are a week behind from the start.

Third, suppliers may be unreliable and inconsistent. This is a common problem and one that is hard to deal with, especially as you may have to appease angry customers who don't really believe that it's not your fault.

All of the above happen every day. Customers do have high expectations in terms of delivery. Everyone wants everything yesterday. You may need to review your operation to ensure that these problems don't occur. Be honest with your customers and don't make promises that you can't keep. If you find that there is going to be a problem with supply, contact the customer to let them know. There is nothing worse than making a special visit to a business to pick up your goods, only to find that they haven't arrived as promised.

Delivering on time is also very relevant for restaurants and professional services. People have a threshold and they don't like to be kept waiting. It's better to advise them of potential delays so that they can decide if they want to wait or not. Better to lose them this time around than to lose them forever because you kept them waiting for three hours. I have a doctor that

I visit and his receptionist rings me prior to the appointment to let me know if he is running on time. This is a great service and it ensures that I don't sit in his waiting room for hours on end. The surgery is only a five-minute drive away, so I can keep working until I get the call that he will soon be available to see me. How many hours have you spent waiting in a doctor's or dentist's surgery?

Time is precious for all of us. Showing that you respect your customers' time is a very important way of distinguishing good service from lousy service.

115 Go shopping at the competition

I am a very strong believer in knowing your competitor's product almost as well as you know your own. The only way to do this is to visit their business and look at it from the point of view of a customer. This is an accepted practice. I have had clients who run large supermarkets and once a week they visit the other main supermarkets to see what their competitors are up to. It is all done very openly, as the managers know each other.

The information that this type of activity can produce is very valuable, especially if you can conduct this kind of survey with an open, objective mind. The following list identifies some of the questions that you need to be able to answer after the survey:

- Is their business easier to find than yours?
- Is it easier to park?
- Is the business more inviting and visually appealing than yours?
- Is the layout more effective?
- How does their range of products compare to yours?
- How do your prices compare?
- Is their business clean?
- How are their staff presented?
- Are the staff friendly and polite?
- Were there long delays in being served?

Some of the above topics may not be relevant to your particular business, but I am sure that there are other questions that could be included.

I always recommend to my clients that they spend time getting to know their competitors before they start to review their own business. We recently developed a marketing strategy for the local operations of a large telecommunications company. The first part of the project entailed visiting all of the other mobile phone shops in the area. There were about 30 in total. We asked questions and reviewed all aspects of these businesses and identified several major weaknesses of each shop. By addressing these weaknesses, which had to do mainly with poor selling skills and an almost compulsive desire to bombard customers with hundreds of glossy brochures without actually selling them anything, we could tailor-make a winning strategy for our client that helped it to become very successful.

This leads on to the point about setting up a business in a highly competitive field. The only way that this can really be done successfully is by having a very clear understanding of what your competitors are doing. Put simply, it's often a matter of looking at how the other businesses operate and identifying ways to do it better. This principle has made a lot of people a lot of money over the years.

Reviewing what your competitor's business offers will usually highlight that it isn't about price as much as it's about service.

116 Set up a customer hotline

In keeping with one of the main themes of this book—that good customer service is all about making it easier for your customers to deal with you—let's look now at the concept of a customer hotline. Unfortunately, in many cases the customer hotline should be renamed the customer 'slow line'. We are all aware of the frustration of calling a customer hotline, only to be told by a mechanised voice that our call is important before then being kept waiting for up to an hour before we get to speak with a real person. As customers we are becoming less tolerant of this form of very bad customer service. It's insulting, especially when the company that you are calling is making billions of dollars and you have to keep handing over your money.

The concept of a customer hotline is simply to provide answers to questions, to enable people to buy a product, and to act as a point of reference and reassurance which customers can use if they need to. If your telephones are always busy, there is the possibility that you are losing a lot of sales simply because people can't get through or they are tired of being put on hold. Some businesses may have a sales hotline and a service hotline. Differentiating the two will enable better priority management, although in the true sense of customer service both lines should be equally important. (Here's a tip: if ever you find yourself waiting in a mechanised queue, just press the option that involves sales and you will be put through to a person much faster.)

For many businesses, having a customer hotline looks professional and gives the customer a sense of reassurance that, after they have handed over their money, they will still be looked after. From a customer service point of view, the risk is reduced and the customer feels more secure when making a purchase.

Several businesses could combine forces to provide a joint customer service hotline to answer enquiries about each business. The main point here is that your customers will have one telephone number that they can ring to get information or to make a purchase.

If you decide to set up a customer hotline, make sure that you tell your customers about it and explain how it works.

117 Simplify your paperwork

I am often amazed by how hard some businesses make it for people to deal with them. This is reflected in the use of over-complicated, hard-to-use and impossible-to-understand paper-work. Such paperwork and forms have often evolved over time. Things have been added but nothing has been removed, and no one has sat down and looked at ways to improve the system.

I recommend that every business should review its forms and paperwork at least once a year. Make sure that it is simple to use—give a sample of your new layout to a friend who doesn't really understand your business and see if they can fill out the form easily. If they can't, how can your customers? Take out anything that is unnecessary or outdated, and if you have to add anything, keep it to a minimum.

We all need to take a very active stance to reduce compli-cated paperwork. For a lot of people, complicated forms are enough of a reason not to buy a product. Imagine how people who have difficulty with reading and writing must feel when they are handed a twenty-page application form.

Look at all of your business's paperwork. Every form should be reviewed periodically and made easier to use. Your customers will definitely appreciate it and so will your bottom line.

118 Using reply paid mail

Research shows that including an envelope with a reply paid address will dramatically increase your success rate when selling products by direct mail. It will also increase your return rate when sent out with accounts. All that it costs you is the postage and the cost of an envelope, yet very few small businesses use this simple promotional and customer service-oriented tool.

As mentioned in other tips throughout this book, a key principle of customer service is making it easy for your customers to deal with you. Saving them time and money are two of the best ways to have your customers coming back for more. In this case, they don't have to find an envelope, then try to find the address that they have to send it to, then find a stamp and finally put the lot together. All they have to do is slip the information into the envelope provided and drop it into the post box next time they are passing by. Beautiful.

119 Start a local campaign encouraging customer service

Why not look at spreading the word about customer service to other businesses—in fact, to entire communities? Some people may think that this would give them less of a competitive advantage in their business environment, and they would probably be right. However, when we look at the bigger picture, if people are coming to a particular destination to buy products and to do business, there is a far greater chance that they will keep coming back if their total experience is memorable.

Imagine visiting a shopping centre where the level of service in all of the businesses that you shopped at was excellent. The staff were all very friendly, professional and well-presented, and they asked you the right questions and provided the products that you needed. If this happened in one shop, you would notice and remember that business. How would you feel if the level of service was equally as good in *all* of the other businesses? Imagine the reputation that this shopping centre would develop. Imagine the number of customers that would keep coming back.

Tourism and hospitality-based areas are perfect for this concept. It is very important that visitors are well treated and given high levels of customer service so that when they go home and tell their friends, colleagues and families about their choice of holiday destination, they give glowing reports and encourage other people to visit the same destination.

By being a customer service champion, you can drive this message home to your local council, business organisations, chambers of commerce and so on. Businesses could be awarded recognition for outstanding levels of service; they could even be rated, like hotels, on the customer service that they provide. All the members of such a collective could have a sign in their windows showing their support of and commitment to customer service.

Look towards the future today. Customer service is going to

become more and more important. The sooner we all start to aspire to higher levels of customer service, the sooner the results will begin to show.

120 Introduce a free service

The introduction of a free service, as compared to a free product, has many advantages for both the customer and the business offering the service. A law firm client of ours offered all of their clients a free key recovery service. Each of their clients was given a key tag with a unique number engraved on it. The tag had the return address for the keys, which was the law firm, also engraved on the back, so that if someone found the keys all they had to do was put them in any post box and the keys would be returned to the law firm, who could then look up the number, identify the client and advise them that their keys had been found. This was a classic win–win situation for both parties and excellent advertising and word-of-mouth promotion for the law firm.

We offer all of our clients a free service where they can contact our business at any time to ask for specific marketing advice. Of course they pay for our main services, but we invite them to call us whenever they have a question or an idea that they would like to run by us. This encourages our clients to stay in touch and it helps to develop a strong, long-term relationship.

The hair salon that my wife visits offers a free follow-up call one week after a cut. She can drop back in and the salon staff will make sure that the style sits right and looks perfect. This great service keeps all of their customers coming back for more.

There are many forms that a free service can take. Most of the time they don't cost a lot of money to implement, but there is no doubt that your customers will appreciate your efforts and will tell their friends. Have a look at your business and try to identify the types of free services that you could implement.

121 Don't let customer service stop when you are busy

We all get busy from time to time. The telephone rings non-stop, there is smoke coming out of the fax machine and the customers are charging through the door, all on the day that someone is off sick. It's great to be this busy, but it's also a time when customer service can really suffer. There can be longer than normal delays, tempers can become strained, you can run out of products, the rubbish bins overflow, and so on. As consumers we understand and accept that when a business is busier than usual, the level of customer service tends to suffer. However, the real problem with businesses that face fluctuating numbers of customers is that the entire focus of the business revolves around the busy times, not the quieter, more normal times, so the entire level of customer service drops.

Several years ago I had a restaurant as a client. They were very busy during the tourism season, which lasted for about three months. For the other nine months of the year they were much quieter, only serving about one-third of the number of diners each day. A mentality had developed in the staff and management that revolved around the three busy months—the rest of the year wasn't taken as seriously. So, for nine months of the year the service was fairly average and for three months it was good. I had to work hard to change this mentality and remind them that it was essential that their levels of service increased during the off season to ensure the long-term growth of the business. However, as soon as attention was diverted from this ongoing re-education, the old philosophy returned.

Just because you are busy today doesn't mean that you will be busy tomorrow. If a competitor moves in and their products or services are as good as yours and their prices similar, but their customer service is better than yours, you are heading into dangerous waters. Be constantly aware of increasing your level of customer service. Don't slacken off because last week was really busy and you want to take it easier this week. Don't stop doing the little things that make your business not just good, but exceptional.

From my experience, when a business stops focusing attention on customer service, the overall level of service drops rapidly, along with the level of customer satisfaction. The financial impact of this is soon evident and very hard to overcome. As with most business maladies, prevention is better than trying to find a cure.

Notes

Customer Service Action List

Things to do   **Completed**

1.

2.

3.

4.

5.

6.

7.

8.

9.

10.

Appendix: Blank forms that may come in handy

The following forms have been designed to illustrate a number of ideas raised in this book. Feel free to adapt them for use in your business.

Your mission to customer service
What do your customers expect from you?
Competitor analysis form
Customer satisfaction survey
Customer service and the telephone
Customer service audit checklist
Ten common customer service mistakes
Ten secrets of customer service success
The little things (what can you do above and beyond
    the call of duty?)
Your customer complaint procedures

Your mission to customer service

Every business needs a policy to define their commitment to customer service. It will let both your customers and your staff know the importance that you place on offering high levels of customer service.

I recommend filling in the following table to help your mission to customer service become clearer in your own mind and the minds of your staff. Make sure that everyone reads this form.

Our mission to customer service

How do you personally feel about your customers?

....

....

Why do your existing customers use your business now?

....

....

What are you going to do to keep your customers coming back?

....

....

How do you want your staff to treat your customers?

....

....

What reputation do you want your business to have when it comes to customer service?

....

....

What do your customers expect from you?

Obtaining a better understanding of customer expectations can be achieved in a number of ways. This form suggests questions that can be asked to help identify what your customers expect from your organisation. The form can be adapted to suit any business and the questions can be asked face-to-face when the customer visits your business, over the telephone, or even by mail. Knowing what your customers want means that you can meet and, where possible, exceed these expectations.

Dear Customer,

We have developed this questionnaire to help our organisation gain a clearer understanding of what your needs and expectations are from our business.

Please rate the following in terms of importance to you:

Aspect of business	Very important	Average	Not important
Ease of parking	☐	☐	☐
Convenient location	☐	☐	☐
Range of products	☐	☐	☐
Layout of the shop	☐	☐	☐
Our trading hours	☐	☐	☐
Our prices	☐	☐	☐
The appearance of our staff	☐	☐	☐
Overall level of customer service	☐	☐	☐
Speed at which you are served	☐	☐	☐
Refund policy	☐	☐	☐
Payment options	☐	☐	☐

If there was one aspect of our business that we could improve upon, what would it be?

....

....

Do you shop at businesses similar to ours
on a regular basis?   ☐ Yes   ☐ No

Which businesses? ....

....

Generally, how do we rate when
compared to them?   ☐ Far better
                            ☐ Better
                            ☐ About the same
                            ☐ Worse
                            ☐ Much worse

Are there any specific reasons why you use our business?

....

....

Competitor analysis form

Understanding the competition is critical when it comes to satisfying your customers. Use this form to highlight areas in which your business needs to improve, as well as showcasing the areas in which your business already outperforms your competitors. These points can then be promoted as reasons why customers should use your business over the competition. Remember, you need to be objective when doing this type of analysis. A scoring system works well as it is less emotive than the Q&A format. Five is the highest (good) score and one is the lowest (poor).

Areas to compare	Competitor One	Competitor Two	Your business
Was it easy to find the telephone number?	5 4 3 2 1	5 4 3 2 1	5 4 3 2 1
Telephone manner of staff?	5 4 3 2 1	5 4 3 2 1	5 4 3 2 1
Overall level of telephone service?	5 4 3 2 1	5 4 3 2 1	5 4 3 2 1
Overall appearance of business?	5 4 3 2 1	5 4 3 2 1	5 4 3 2 1
Is it easy to find?	5 4 3 2 1	5 4 3 2 1	5 4 3 2 1
Is it easy to park?	5 4 3 2 1	5 4 3 2 1	5 4 3 2 1
Is the business inviting?	5 4 3 2 1	5 4 3 2 1	5 4 3 2 1
First impressions?	5 4 3 2 1	5 4 3 2 1	5 4 3 2 1
Is the business well laid out?	5 4 3 2 1	5 4 3 2 1	5 4 3 2 1
Are the staff well presented?	5 4 3 2 1	5 4 3 2 1	5 4 3 2 1
Is it easy to find what you are looking for?	5 4 3 2 1	5 4 3 2 1	5 4 3 2 1
Are the staff helpful?	5 4 3 2 1	5 4 3 2 1	5 4 3 2 1
Is it clean and tidy?	5 4 3 2 1	5 4 3 2 1	5 4 3 2 1

Is it easy to make a purchase?	5 4 3 2 1	5 4 3 2 1	5 4 3 2 1
How was the noise level?	5 4 3 2 1	5 4 3 2 1	5 4 3 2 1
Did the staff look at you?	5 4 3 2 1	5 4 3 2 1	5 4 3 2 1
Did they thank you?	5 4 3 2 1	5 4 3 2 1	5 4 3 2 1
Were the staff friendly?	5 4 3 2 1	5 4 3 2 1	5 4 3 2 1
Was the waiting time to get served OK?	5 4 3 2 1	5 4 3 2 1	5 4 3 2 1
How was the pricing?	5 4 3 2 1	5 4 3 2 1	5 4 3 2 1
....	5 4 3 2 1	5 4 3 2 1	5 4 3 2 1
....	5 4 3 2 1	5 4 3 2 1	5 4 3 2 1
....	5 4 3 2 1	5 4 3 2 1	5 4 3 2 1
....	5 4 3 2 1	5 4 3 2 1	5 4 3 2 1

Customer satisfaction survey

Customer satisfaction surveys are not complicated or difficult to put into place—all they take is a little bit of time, honest questions and a willingness to want to know the answers. Keep questions short and to the point so that answers can be given simply and clearly. Like all of the blank forms in this book, it is recommended that you adapt it to suit your own business with questions that are relevant to the products or services that you sell.

Customer satisfaction survey

Was it easy to find our business?
☐ Yes   ☐ No

How is the appearance of our business?
☐ Excellent   ☐ Good   ☐ Average   ☐ Poor

How would you rate the cleanliness?
☐ Excellent   ☐ Good   ☐ Average   ☐ Poor

How is the atmosphere (noise, smells, etc.)?
☐ Excellent   ☐ Good   ☐ Average   ☐ Poor

Did you telephone before you visited?
☐ Yes   ☐ No

How would you rate the level of telephone service?
☐ Excellent   ☐ Good   ☐ Average   ☐ Poor

How would you rate our products/services?
☐ Excellent   ☐ Good   ☐ Average   ☐ Poor

Would you purchase them again?
☐ Yes   ☐ No   ☐ Unsure

How would you rate our pricing?
☐ Excellent   ☐ Good   ☐ Average   ☐ Poor

How was the overall level of customer service?
☐ Excellent   ☐ Good   ☐ Average   ☐ Poor

How would you rate the appearance of the staff?
☐ Excellent   ☐ Good   ☐ Average   ☐ Poor

How would you rate their level of professionalism?

☐ Excellent ☐ Good ☐ Average ☐ Poor

Did you find the staff friendly?

☐ Yes ☐ No ☐ Unsure

Would you use our business again?

☐ Yes ☐ No ☐ Unsure

Would you recommend our business to your friends?

☐ Yes ☐ No ☐ Unsure

What did you like most about our business?

....

....

....

What did you like least about our business?

....

....

....

Do you have any suggestions for improving our business?

....

....

....

Customer service and the telephone

Telephone technique is often overlooked when discussing customer service but it is an integral component of the entire customer–business interaction. We all spend more and more time on the telephone and now, more than ever, the importance of quality customer service on the telephone is being realised. This form has been prepared to enable you to review your telephone customer service and to look for ways to improve the level of service offered and, ultimately, to really satisfy your customers.

Yes	No	Telephone service audit
☐	☐	Is it easy to find the telephone number of the business?
☐	☐	Is the number easy to remember?
☐	☐	If calling from out of town, does the business have a toll free number?
☐	☐	Is the call answered quickly?
☐	☐	Is the greeting friendly?
☐	☐	Can you hear the person clearly?
☐	☐	Can they answer your questions?
☐	☐	Do they give you 100 per cent of their attention?
☐	☐	If you are put on hold, is the music too loud or inappropriate?
☐	☐	Is your call returned promptly (if applicable)?
☐	☐	If calling out of hours, is there an answering machine to take a message?
☐	☐	If you are transferred, are you cut off?
☐	☐	Did you have to continually explain your request to different people in the business?
☐	☐	Did you hang up satisfied that this is the business for you to use?

Follow-up required

....

....

....

....

....

....

....

....

....

Customer service audit checklist

Throughout this book a lot of emphasis has been placed on the importance of finding ways to improve a business's overall level of customer service. A very good exercise is to conduct your own customer service audit, the aim of which is to review your current procedures and look for ways to improve the level of service that you offer. This form highlights the areas that need to be audited. Tailor your own customer service audit checklist around this form and conduct an audit as soon as you can.

Yes	No	**From the outside looking in**
☐	☐	Is it easy for customers to find the business?
☐	☐	Are parking facilities acceptable?
☐	☐	Is the lighting adequate?
☐	☐	Is the front of the business inviting?
☐	☐	Is the sign-writing of a high standard?
☐	☐	Is the entrance to the building clean?
☐	☐	Are there any obstructions to the business entrance?

		Inside the business
☐	☐	Is the business clean and tidy?
☐	☐	Is it well laid out?
☐	☐	Do the staff greet the customers as they enter?
☐	☐	Is the telephone answered promptly?
☐	☐	Is the telephone manner of a high standard?
☐	☐	Is it easy for customers to find their way around the business?
☐	☐	Are products well labelled?
☐	☐	Are the staff well presented?
☐	☐	Are the staff knowledgeable?
☐	☐	Are the customers served quickly?
☐	☐	Can customers be served faster?

Yes	No	
☐	☐	Is it easy for customers to pay for their purchases?
☐	☐	Is the level of service consistent?
☐	☐	Are customers given customer satisfaction surveys?
☐	☐	Are the results of these collated?

Behind the scenes

Yes	No	
☐	☐	Are telephone calls returned quickly?
☐	☐	Are emails responded to quickly?
☐	☐	Are orders dispatched quickly?
☐	☐	Are the products well packaged?
☐	☐	Are invoices sent promptly?
☐	☐	Are bills paid promptly?

Ten common customer service mistakes

Identifying the common areas in which customer service does not meet the expectations of the customer can help you avoid those mistakes in your own business. I strongly suggest that you look through the list below and honestly appraise your own business. If your business is guilty of making some mistakes don't beat yourself up, just start working towards eliminating them. I also recommend that a copy of this list be given to all staff so that they can conduct a self-evaluation too.

The ten most common customer service mistakes

	Yes	No	Possibly
1. A lack of respect for the customer's time—always late, rushing, etc.	☐	☐	☐
2. Making promises and not delivering.	☐	☐	☐
3. Becoming too familiar—crossing boundaries.	☐	☐	☐
4. Poor communication skills (lack of ability to talk to customers).	☐	☐	☐
5. Airing company grievances to the customer.	☐	☐	☐
6. Inconsistent service (good one day, bad the next).	☐	☐	☐
7. Changing staff frequently—customer loses desire to form relationship.	☐	☐	☐
8. Poor complaint resolution skills.	☐	☐	☐
9. Customer is taken for granted.	☐	☐	☐
10. Not following up on a sale—how is it going?	☐	☐	☐

Ten secrets of customer service success

Just as it is important to know the most common mistakes when it comes to customer service, knowing and understanding the secrets to customer service success can be a powerful tool. Make it a goal to go through each secret, review it, and look for ways to make it a reality in your business. Likewise, give each member of staff a copy to show them what you are trying to achieve.

Of course, there are many other important factors when it comes to customer service success and these have been discussed in this book. But if you follow the ten key points below your business will stand out from the crowd as a provider of quality customer service—and your customers will keep coming back.

The ten secrets of customer service success

1. Always treat your customers with respect—respect their time, their decision to shop at your business, their privacy, etc.
2. If you make a promise, deliver—no buts and no exceptions. Learn to make realistic promises.
3. Let your customer set the boundaries in terms of familiarity.
4. If you are not a good communicator, work on developing these skills (learn to listen).
5. All dirty washing (internal company problems) must stay out of conversations with customers—they don't want to know and you shouldn't be telling them.
6. Offer a consistent level of service—day in and day out.
7. Keep staff changes to a minimum and have structured handover periods to minimise disruption to customers.
8. Learn to sell. A good salesperson is a good customer service person—the two go hand in hand.
9. Never take the customer for granted.
10. Continue to treat the customer like a new customer (the honeymoon never ends).

The little things (what can you do above and beyond the call of duty?)

I suggest that you sit down with your team, or even friends and family and other business associates, and have a brainstorming session about ways that your business can offer better levels of customer service. The aim is to look for the little things that will make your business stand out from the crowd and develop a reputation as a quality service provider. The following list is designed to get the brainstorming session going. The points identified can be discussed openly with general debate about the current procedure, followed by ideas and suggestions for ways to go above and beyond the call of duty.

Topics for discussion (work through one per week)

- ☐ The appearance of the business.
- ☐ The lighting outside and inside the business.
- ☐ The ambience (noise, smells, etc.).
- ☐ Cleanliness of the business.
- ☐ Layout of the business.
- ☐ The flow of customers through the business.
- ☐ Telephone manner—is it as good as it can be?
- ☐ The greeting of customers.
- ☐ Looking after customers when they are inside the business.
- ☐ Do the staff go out of their way to help customers?
- ☐ Are there ways to speed up service?
- ☐ Are there ways to make it easier for customers to buy from the business?
- ☐ Is the packaging practical and can it be improved?
- ☐ Is the dispatch system friendly and personal?
- ☐ Do we have good relationships with customers?
- ☐ Any ideas or suggestions for improving customer service?

Your customer complaint procedures

This form can be reproduced and edited to make it applicable to your business. The aim of having a structured complaint resolution procedure is to ensure that any complaints that arise are handled in a professional and fair manner for all parties involved.

If you are unable to resolve the situation, you may have to consider legal action. This is not an ideal situation, but it does remove the emotional aspect of the dispute.

It is important that all staff be made aware of how customer complaints are to be handled—remember that the reputation of your company is at stake.

Customer notifies you of a complaint	Remain calm. Listen to the customer. Write down their name. Be patient and understanding. Ask the customer how they would like to see the problem resolved. Decide on a course of action and advise superiors if necessary. Explain to the customer what you will be doing to assist with their complaint. If possible resolve the complaint immediately.
If it cannot be resolved on the spot	Let the customer know exactly what you will be doing and when you will be doing it. Make certain that the right people are advised of the complaint. Stay in touch with the customer as promised.

	If other staff are brought into the dispute make sure they are kept up-to-date. Work towards a fair resolution for both parties. Keep records of all discussions and telephone calls.
If it still cannot be resolved	Look at getting a third party to mediate on the complaint. Stay in touch with the customer. Look for ways to resolve the problem.

A final note from the author

I hope that after reading this book you will be a dedicated advocate of customer service. I also hope that you have developed an understanding of how customer service can impact your business, both positively and negatively. The greatest observation that I have made in this field is that truly successful businesses have a very firm and clear commitment to offering the highest levels of service possible to each and every one of their customers. It doesn't mean that they always get it right, but even when they do get it wrong they still manage to make it right with their customers. Stay in touch with your customers, do the little things that other businesses don't do, constantly review your business through the eyes of your customers, and be consistent. If you focus on these issues I have no doubt that your business will stand out from the crowd and succeed, and that your customers will keep coming back for more.

Andrew Griffiths

Recommended reading

Carnegie, D., 1981, *How to Win Friends and Influence People*, Harper Collins, New York

Finch, L., 1994, *Twenty Ways to Improve Customer Service*, Crisp Publications, New York

Griffiths, A., 2000, *101 Ways to Market Your Business*, Allen & Unwin, Sydney

Griffiths, A., 2002, *101 Survival Tips for Your Business*, Allen & Unwin, Sydney

Gross, S., 1991, *Positively Outrageous Service*, Warner Books, New York

Kaufman, R., 2000, *Up Your Service*, Ron Kaufman Pte Ltd, Singapore

About the author

Andrew Griffiths is an entrepreneur with a passion for small business. From humble beginnings as an orphan growing up in Western Australia, Andrew has owned and operated a number of successful small businesses, starting with his first enterprise—a newspaper round—at age seven. Since then Andrew has sold encyclopaedias door-to-door, travelled the world as an international sales manager, worked in the Great Sandy Desert for a gold exploration company and been a commercial diver. Clearly this unusual menagerie of experiences have made him the remarkable man he is.

Inspired by his desire to see others reach their goals, Andrew has written five hugely successful books with many more on the way. His 101 series offers small business owners practical and achievable advice. The series is sold in over forty countries worldwide.

Andrew is the founding director of The Marketing Professionals, one of Australia's best and most respected marketing and business development firms. Producing innovative solutions to common business issues, The Marketing Professionals advises both large and small business.

Known for his ability to entertain, inspire and deliver key messages, Andrew is also a powerful motivational speaker who brings flamboyancy and verve to the corporate keynote-speaking circuit.

All of this occurs from his chosen home of Cairns, North Queensland, the Great Barrier Reef, Australia.

To read more about Andrew Griffiths visit:
www.andrewgriffiths.com.au
www.themarketingprofessionals.com.au
www.enhanceplus.com.au

101 WAYS TO MARKET YOUR BUSINESS

Stand out from the crowd

Here are 101 practical marketing suggestions to help you achieve dramatic improvements in your business without investing a lot of time and money.

Simple, affordable and quick these innovative tips are easy to implement and will bring you fast results. Choose and apply at least one new idea each week or use this book as a source of inspiration for new ways to market your services, your products and your business itself.

With tips designed to take just a few moments to read *101 Ways to Market Your Business* will help you find new customers, increase the loyalty of the customers you already have, create great promotional material and make your business stand out from the crowd.

INCLUDES 20 BONUS SUGGESTIONS TO HELP YOU ATTRACT NEW CUSTOMERS AND KEEP YOUR EXISTING ONES

101 WAYS TO BOOST YOUR BUSINESS

Energise your business today

Here are 101 powerful tips to kick-start your business and unlock some of the potential that may be struggling to break through.

Written in no-nonsense language and designed to take just a few moments to read each tip, *101 Ways to Boost Your Business* shows you how to make your business better and ultimately more profitable. With tips that can be actioned immediately, you will see results quickly.

These tips cover a host of everyday business issues and are equally applicable to all industries in each and every corner of the world. They will save you thousands of dollars.

INCLUDES 20 BONUS TIPS THAT WILL RECHARGE YOUR BUSINESS

101 WAYS TO ADVERTISE YOUR BUSINESS

Read this before you spend another cent on advertising

Here are 101 proven tips to increase the effectiveness of your advertising. Use these tips to understand what makes one ad work while another fails and you will save a small fortune in wasted advertising.

With tips designed to take just a few moments to read, *101 Ways to Advertise Your Business* offers step-by-step advice on how to make an advertisement, how to buy advertising space and how to make sure that your advertisement is working to its full potential. Follow the tips and your business will soon be reaping the benefits.

INCLUDES A SPECIAL BONUS SECTION CONTAINING HUNDREDS OF THE BEST ADVERTISING WORDS AND PHRASES